The Percy Graeme Turnbull
Memorial Lectures on Poetry
1961

The Percy Graeme Turnbull
Memorial Lectures on Poetry

*Delivered at The Johns Hopkins University
and published by The Johns Hopkins Press*

1951. E. M. W. Tillyard, THE ENGLISH RENAISSANCE: FACT OR FICTION (1952).

1957. Richmond Lattimore, THE POETRY OF GREEK TRAGEDY (1958).

1958. Don Cameron Allen, ed., FOUR POETS ON POETRY (1959).

1961. Don Cameron Allen, ed., THE MOMENT OF POETRY (1962).

The Moment of Poetry

The Moment
of
Poetry

EDITED BY

Don Cameron Allen

THE JOHNS HOPKINS PRESS : BALTIMORE

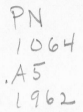

Copyright © 1962 by The Johns Hopkins Press, Baltimore, Md. 21218

Printed in the United States of America

Library of Congress Catalog Card Number 62–12569

Originally published, 1962

Second printing, 1967

The editor is grateful to the following publishers for permission to reprint materials originally published by them: to Grove Press, Inc., for Edwin Muir's "The Combat" from *Collected Poems, 1921-1951*; to Harms, Inc. for "It's Only a Paper Moon," © 1933 by Harms, Inc., and used by permission; to Harvard University Press for quotations from Ben Shahn's *The Shape of Content*, © 1957 by the President and Fellows of Harvard College; to Holt, Rinehart & Winston, Inc., for Robert Frost's "Home Burial" from *Complete Poems of Robert Frost*, © 1930, 1939 by Holt, Rinehart & Winston, Inc., for A. E. Housman's "1887" and "On the Idle Hill of Summer" from "A Shropshire Lad"–authorized edition–published in *Complete Poems*, © 1959 by Holt, Rinehart & Winston, Inc., and for his "Epitaph on an Army of Mercenaries" from *Last Poems*, © 1922 by Holt, Rinehart & Winston, Inc., © renewed 1950 by Barclays Bank, Ltd.; to Alfred A. Knopf, Inc., for John Crow Ransom's "Painted Head" from *Selected Poems*, 1945; to Little, Brown & Co. for Ogden Nash's "Reflections on Ice-Breaking," reprinted by permission of the author; first published in The New Yorker; © 1930 by Ogden Nash; © renewed 1957 by Ogden Nash; to the Macmillan Co. for W. B. Yeats's "A Bronze Head" and "A King and No King" from *Collected Poems*, 1933; to Pantheon Books, Inc., for quotations from Eugen Herrigel's *Zen in the Art of Archery*; and to G. P. Putnam's Sons for Thomas Blackburn's "The School of Babylon" from *The Next Word*.

Contents

Introduction

THOSE OF US WHO BELIEVE THAT poetry is a form of knowledge and that the poet's mode of thinking is a valid means of understanding the mortal world, where what is called "rational agreement" is simply agreement, have always found of extraordinary importance the comments of poets on themselves, on other poets, and on poetry. It is, indeed, pleasant to discover how acceptable this conclusion has become in the world of learning. Most American colleges and universities now assume that the actual presence of the artist's living imagination is as essential to their intellectual life—and hence to that of the nation—as the scholar's discriminating memory and the scientist's mathematical logic. Unlike most of their European counterparts, few distinguished American places of higher learning welcome and honor the academician with no skill in either words or colors, who discourses on literature and art, and exclude the true man of letters or art. Poets of reputation and achievement are now the cherished inhabitants of many American campuses. Here they are not required, as sometimes they are abroad, to hide their talents under the mask of a scientist or scholar; they may follow their proper bents by cultivating their own artistic powers and by bringing to fruition the talents of younger people. Though not unknown custom in the last century when few American poets went in want, the happy admission of the poet to the university faculty is one of the more noble aspects of our contemporary culture.

The Johns Hopkins University, which named the poet Sidney Lanier to its first faculty, has always subscribed to the doctrine that poetry is a way of seeking the truth that sets men free. In accordance with this belief, it brought to its halls during the last week of October, 1961, the group of distinguished American poets whose talks I am honored to publish in this volume. In the first, John Holmes, Professor of English at Tufts College and author of many books of verse and books about verse, describes, by expanding his metaphor of Stonehenge, the poet's milieu, the things that stand round the poet and make him poet. Miss May Sarton, author since 1938 of six books of verse and seven novels, modestly disavows her critical powers and then proceeds to tell us, as she has often told her students at Wellesley College, how a poet works. In the third essay, Richard Eberhart, Professor of English at Dartmouth, whose *Collected Poems, 1930-1960* have just been published, distinguishes between two aspects of poetic thought which he defines as "will" and "psyche." All of these poets talk about other poets, but the poets Randall Jarrell and Richard Wilbur center their critical imaginations on definite poems. Mr. Wilbur, Professor of English at Connecticut Wesleyan and the most brilliant poet of the new generation, shows us that we require more than naked wit to understand what seems at first a simple lyric satire. In the like vein, Randall Jarrell, Professor at the Woman's College of the University of North Carolina, novelist, and translator, whose recent *Woman at the Washington Zoo* won the National Book Award, shows us how to find our way through the not immediately visible artistic complications of one of Robert Frost's great poems.

We can only hope that these essays will find as many enthusiastic readers as they had hearers. But they can hardly go forth without the editor acknowledging the help that made them possible. First, he should like to thank the members of the Turnbull family of Baltimore whose gift in memory of a talented man, Percy Graeme Turnbull, endowed these lectures, the Turnbull Memorial Lectures. Next, he is extremely thankful to the Bollingen Foundation of New York City, whose generous grant once again made another Johns Hopkins Poetry Festival possible.

DON CAMERON ALLEN

BALTIMORE, 1961

John Holmes

Surroundings
and
Illuminations

THE POET IS NOT POET OF HIM-self alone, except in that last hour when he writes his poem. The poet writing, and the poet living his ordinary days, is ringed about by powers and influences. Whether he is affected by them, or with full awareness rejects them, the poet is a center of surroundings and illuminations. From the outside it may seem like Robert Frost's couplet, "We dance around in a ring and suppose, But the Secret sits in the middle and knows." To make possible more than supposing, and to remind the poet, who is the Secret, I propose a metaphor of Stonehenge. There were three of them. We know the ruins of mystery in the rings, and the one thing we instinctively suppose is that there is a Secret in the middle of it.

Four thousand years ago, herdsmen from the Continent made Stonehenge I, a corral and butchering-place. The outermost ring, three hundred feet in diameter, was a ditch eight feet deep, its earth heaped in a bank at the inner edge, to keep cattle. Stonehenge II was a temple built inside the ancient corrals, by another population from across the Channel, two thousand years later. These people dug a ring of graves just inside the bank, filled it in time with cremated bones, bronze spear-tips from Ireland, amber beads from Europe, gold jewelry from Greece. The third wave of settlers set up two inner rings of pillarlike bluestone, brought with long toil from Wales by raft and roller. This was Stonehenge III, the one we know the ruins of. About 1500 B.C., sandstone slabs, shaped and brought from twenty miles away, were set up in a hundred-foot temple circle. Close inside them, the bluestone pillars from older rings were reset, and inside that a sandstone horseshoe around another of bluestone. The opening of the horseshoe, with certain guidestones, is toward the rising of the sun on Midsummer Day, June 24. At the center is a sixteen-foot block of sandstone, an altar; but in the metaphor I propose, that is where the poet sits, ringed round by more past than he knows.

I intend to make the Stonehenge metaphor work for me, not employ me. There are direct and meaningful likenesses. There are the recovered pillars out of the past, used again. There is the never-forgotten direction toward the sun. There are the barrows, layered with those objects that outlast man; tools; small, hard works of art; and bones of the body. And there is the evidence of incredible effort, generations of inexhaustible labor, and triumphs of constructive cunning. None of this was local. It was a time of translation, of interchange of skill and subject, a busy time of trading and exploiting. The archeological fact I like best is proof that the master planner and overseer of Stonehenge III was Greek. Someone knew how to bulge the huge pillars, and cut the lintel-stones wider at the top, for an optical illusion of straightness. Someone made mortise-and-tenon joints. Ten years ago, a carving on a Stonehenge column of a hilted dagger, of a type made only at Mycenae, only around 1550 B.C., was found, and made positive the presence far away and long ago of Greece in early England. One marvels and is reassured. It was the signature of an artist that outlasted. But my introductory image is not of antique and ruined stone. It is of an equivalent for the infinitely rich and available past, always nearer and always more available than we think, thanks to Celts and Greeks. There stand the rings, at any rate, of temple stones, of burial-holes, and earth walls against the wilderness, and in the center the Secret, the Poet. The surroundings I mean now are of active intelligence recording, evaluating, and discoursing upon poetry, and the illuminations I mean are of the perpetuators who love, and teach, and explain poetry.

It is with these that I shall deal, reminding more than informing, and by reminding, renew only once more, after all the renewals, the great inflowing and outreaching forces that prolong poetry's life. The poets are surrounded as they live and work, by presences of poets past and contemporary; by biographers; by reviewers and critics; by teachers; by editors and publishers; and by listeners and readers, that is, by audiences.

That there are wide waiting circles older than the oldest poet living, and as new as the newest first book, no poet is wholly aware. And he should not be very much aware; not when he is writing. If the poet looked up and around for approval, or veto, or help, it could turn into a nightmare of self-consciousness. He must balance an arrogant unawareness with a magnificent awareness, such a split personality as the actor knows, playing his part alone in a full theater. "One ruthless purpose, and that purpose poetry," is the secret the poet knows, sitting there in the middle of the ancient rings. Tradition, the monumental and hard-weathered past, is there to be used, stones as books to be rebuilt in the new temple. Stonehenge is his example even for building with old stone for new purpose; even when it is done in creative revolt; even in ignorance. Historical man is stronger than living man. The poet knows this, too. This is the Secret he finally cannot keep from himself, the ultimate mystery. My argument is that these other books, these companies and hosts at the ritual of writing the poem, do not interfere with, or become substitutes for, or in any way thin or distort, the poetry itself. Instead, they take up poetry's life and carry it outward, prolonging it in time, adding to it weight and worth it hardly had when it was new.

II

Some of those giant, silent figures standing out there in the dark are the poets, not stern and admonishing, and not benevolently nodding, either; but there. They are the poets our one poet has read. " Everything must ring like Elizabethan English," wrote Katherine Mansfield in a letter, " and like those gentlemen I always seem to be mentioning, ' the Poets.' There is a light upon them, especially upon the Elizabethans and our special set—Keats, Wordsworth, Coleridge, Shelley, De Quincey, and Co. Those are the people with whom I want to live, those are the men I feel are our brothers." For her they were, but for each poet they will be different. The best that the best of them ever wrote is the mark he tries for, despairingly or hopefully, and then at last with furious indifference. He knows that the least he can do is not shame himself in the eyes of Ben Jonson, who might laugh at him long and loud; or Rilke, who might not even hear him; or Thomas Hardy. How would one know if Thomas Hardy liked one's poem? There was a poet who found out. Charlotte Mew was given by his executor a British Museum Reading Room slip on which he had copied out one of her poems. She died two months later, in 1928, but reading Alida Munro's heartbreaking memoir, one rejoices that she did see that piece of paper. Mostly there is no such narrow margin, or no acknowledgment at all. We hear that Masefield admired Chaucer; that Frost read the Romans and Longfellow; and how many in our times have read and used Dante to powerful and relevant purpose, we know.

But this outer ring of giants is set there by the poet himself. No scholars guess the real influences from the poets to the poet. I can say that one of my giants is John Donne, who used a metaphor of power such as coins, mines, maps, royalty, and the sun, all symbolic of enormously concentrated authority. I like Herrick, but not Byron; Marvell and Campion, but not very much Browning; Blake, Milton, and Marlowe, but not Pope, Swinburne, or Spenser. Nearer the poet are a few poets of his own time. Winfield Townley Scott began so Robinsonian that it seems a miracle he escaped into his own language, one I envy and admire. Charles Olson seems not to have escaped Ezra Pound. Otherwise, how can I know the ring around Elizabeth Bishop, or John Berryman, or Vernon Watkins, poets of my time I much admire? They have their own secrets, as they are part of mine. Another poet whose manners, rhythm, and vocabulary are so pervasive as to stain the style of anyone who touches them is dangerous. Robinson is just such a poet, of course, and Pound, and so are Emily Dickinson, Hopkins, Eliot, and Frost. Who wants to be known as that young poet who writes like Emily Dickinson? I am wary in association with Robert Frost, and have consciously stood out away from his shadow and voice through thirty years of friendship. Like these others, he is one of a kind. I have learned that from him. I owe more to the Celtic wildness and superb formal control of Robert Graves and William Butler Yeats. From Frost I learn management of my life and image, and from hours and hours of talk, his talk, I learn how living a restless mind at play can be. I like the dry, wrenched understatement of John Crowe Ransom; the upper-world infinity of Wallace Stevens, the exclamatory empathy of William Carlos Williams, the delighted honor that Marianne Moore pays to objects, the things of this world.

Among such figures, not influences in the textual sense, not patterns in the imitative sense, is still another kind, what W. H. Auden calls the Master. Auden said, in his Inaugural Lecture at Oxford, in 1956,

> My first Master was Thomas Hardy, and I think I was very lucky in my choice. He was a good poet, perhaps a great one, but not *too* good. Much as I loved him, even I could see that his diction was often clumsy and forced and that a lot of his poems were plain bad. This gave me hope where a flawless poet might have made me despair. He was modern without being too modern. His world and sensibility were close enough to mine—curiously enough his face bore a striking resemblance to my father's—so that in imitating him, I was being led towards, not away from myself, but they were not so close as to obliterate my identity. If I looked through his spectacles, at least I was conscious of a certain eye-strain. Lastly, his metrical variety, his fondness for complicated stanza forms, were an invaluable training in the craft of making. I am thankful also that my first Master did not write in free verse or I might have been tempted to believe that free verse is easier to write than stricter forms, whereas I know it is infinitely more difficult.

So much for one of the rings. It has a much more personal turn than I had expected from my rather ceremonial-sounding metaphor of the Stonehenge circlings, but it is necessarily the one only the poet sees, the shadowy and shifting one, the listeners and watchers imagined by the poet at the center.

III

Henry James wrote a preface to Rupert Brooke's *Letters From America*, a young traveler's journalism. James, the conscious artist, said, " Nothing more generally or more recurrently solicits us, in the light of literature, I think, than the interest of our learning how the poet, the true poet, and above all the particular one with whom for the moment we may be concerned, has come into his estate, asserted and preserved his identity, worked out his question of sticking to that and to nothing else; and has so been able to reach us and touch us *as* a poet, in spite of the accidents and dangers that must have beset this course." Not many biographies of poets are concerned as wholly as Henry James would wish with the life-cycle of the poet's identity. The Rupert Brooke book was a fragment, a secondary document, as most biographies are. They answer more often the question, " Who was he?" than the question, " What was he?" Or if we learn what made him the poet who reaches and touches us as poet, it is because we know beforehand how the game came out. We can say to Keats, " Fool, can't you see you must not waste a year, for money, on a five-act play no one will ever put on? Begin the Odes now!" Reading Philip Horton's life of Hart Crane, we might wish to be on the boat homebound from Cuba, and tell the poet that having no new subsidized manuscript is no reason for jumping overboard. What a roll call of dolor, if every empty-handed foundationer committed honorable hara-kiri! Few poets live heroically to make brave biographies, or if they do, their poetry is probably second-rate. If Leon Edel has his way, and a new form and intention, the literary biography, comes into being, then we may have some monuments for my metaphor.

Yet I believe that poetry is the product of the whole man, not only not isolated from, but in every day nourished by his living. If we learn from the poets' biographies that, like everyone else, they have to do too much of what they have to do, the kind of biography Leon Edel and Henry James want would show us how this, too, made the poems. "The evidence is mulled over," Malcolm Cowley says, "all the details are fitted together until they begin to form a picture, vague and broken at first, then growing more distinct as the years pass by: the X or Y picture, the James Joyce, Paul Valéry, or T. S. Eliot picture. But it is not so much a picture when completed: it is rather a map or diagram which the apprentice will use in planning his own career." And John Crowe Ransom's poem, "Painted Head," while at one level it may be a treatise on portrait-painting, is another piece of evidence for the apprentices, in the poet's way of life:

> The body bears the head
> (So hardly one they terribly are two)
> Feeds and obeys and unto please what end?
> Not to the glory of tyrant head but to
>
> The increase of body. Beauty is of body.
> The flesh contouring shallowly on a head
> Is a rock-garden needing body's love
> And best bodiness . . .

In terms of biography, it says we understand the poetry the head made, the more we know about the life the body lived. Perhaps it is a little advanced for apprentices.

There is no poet's biography of our times to match William Butler Yeats's own life of himself. It was so constructed as to be one-third of his whole life-story, yet a book by itself, as the other two parts, his collected poems, and his collected essays, are books separately. Whichever is read first, the next is brightened by it, and the third by the first two. If a beginner could be advised, I would wish him to read the poems first, then the essays, which are black-and-white versions of the poems' color, and then *Reveries over Childhood and Youth*, and *The Trembling of the Veil*, completed later as *Autobiographies*. Perhaps no other poet's life ever or anywhere is as much worth reading. It is deliberately and magnificently and triply that assertion and preservation of identity that Henry James meant. To be sure, Ellmann, and Fraser, and Hone, and Jaffares tell us things about Yeats that Yeats does not. But when the figure is as great a figure of the artist as Yeats was, we read everything. We even procure the exhibition catalog, *Images of a Poet*, of paintings and photographs, printed books and manuscripts, shown in Manchester and Dublin in the summer of 1961. This is Ransom's rock-garden head and best bodiness indeed.

IV

Who says too much poetry is being written? It cannot really be the magazine editors and book publishers, because they gladly print ten times as much about poets and poetry as they print the poem itself. It would seem that they prefer the established fact, derivative from poetry, to that uncertain, not yet stabilized element, the poem—the new poem. In the terms of my metaphor, editors of magazines must seem the most monolithic of all the surroundings; barrier rather than benevolence. I think that the editorial function is doomed: an editor is a benevolent barrier. In the office of a major magazine other skills than the recognition of good poetry occupy editor's time and thought. A magazine staff is lucky to have one member willing to risk judgment of a poem. The poet's dealings will be with that one person, who will go elsewhere in two or three years. But the poet is lucky to find him, or her: this is one face of the real world.

It is different and far more to the poet's advantage in the literary quarterlies. Poets and critics of poetry read these, and book-publishers scout them. Their pages are the real arena where the important show is going on. The reward is prestige, attention, and reader-writer equivalence; not much cash passes. It is all rather otherworldly, but stimulating, responsive, much to be preferred. Editorial personalities dominate these magazines, and the best of them are warm and perceptive, and all poets come to know some of them. They are responsible to poetry itself, and if they are replaced, it will be by someone very similar.

The game of magazine appearances is so shifting and complex, so rivalrous and egoistic, and played on such a small field, it requires full-time watching with high-power binoculars. It's a good sport, if ego and energy hold out. Four hundred magazines print poems, but to achieve the right dozen for that important list of acknowledgments at the front of a first book, the utmost discretion, effort, and patience are necessary. Most people who write a poem think first of the *Atlantic Monthly* or the *New Yorker*, where the daily mailbags go out one door as fast as they come in another. Space for poetry in the big-circulation magazines steadily decreases, and even the littlest of the little magazines receives more than it can print. I think of poetry editors as distracted hostesses, greeting a totally unexpected guest while eyes flicker over already overcrowded rooms, and they make polite, meaningless remarks; that is to say, rejection slips. But now and then a good host takes charge, like the no-nonsense editor of the *New Orleans Poetry Journal*. Or a good hostess, like Harriet Monroe, who printed, I am sure, poems she did not like and could not really understand, in her magazine, *Poetry: A Magazine of Verse*, because she respected them. There are poetry editors like those, and will always be, I am sure. My metaphor ensures it.

Major book-publishers have a poetry quotient of two or three titles a year. They can afford to lose a little money on the chance of prizes, or for the sake of a balanced list. This is patronage publication, for which we may be as grateful as we may. Some of us turn into real publishers' properties, as they say; but problematical. We must never forget that the poet is not a businessman and that the publisher is not a poet, though both of them get mixed up about it. There are and always have been some brave book-publishers; among whom Alan Swallow of Denver stands high, for his long devotion to poetry. Some of the young houses seem more generously interested in poetry than the old ones. The finest poetry publishing venture in many years is being carried out by the Wesleyan University Press. But great things in poetry can be hoped for from some of the massive paperback publishers, if I read the signs right.

Nevertheless bewilderment is the typical look on the faces of publishers and editors as they stand round about the poets. In the general architectural scheme I describe, this ring stands rather sideways, stone face by stone face, the attention mostly somewhere else. The history of their own lists should prove to publishers that while one poet may be good for two to five books of poems, his future is good for ten or twenty books that will sell better. The complete poetry of Gerard Manley Hopkins makes a book less than one inch thick, but my incomplete shelf of books about Hopkins is two feet long. Yeats, whose own books are many, is stretched out to double his length. Rooms in libraries, whole libraries, are filled with books about Keats and Shakespeare; with decorative extra touches of original manuscript and statuary. The long-delayed complete poems of Emily Dickinson make three volumes; theories of her life are still coming out. I come to attention before the Robinson shelf. The line of his own published verses, narrative poems, and, alas, plays, is still much longer than all the books yet written about him as man and poet. An early appreciation by a Frenchman, Charles Cestre; a bibliography and a doctoral thesis or two; the life by Hermann Hagedorn; some letters, but nowhere near all there are—these, and Lawrance Thompson's inevitable selection, *Tilbury Town*, with its valuable preface, and Ellsworth Barnard's first-rate study of Robinson's total poetry, are little enough. But publishers will fill such lacks, being easier to convince on this than they were on Robinson's first poems. He paid for his own first book.

V

The good critics are the real responsibles in the temple of poetry I have schemed. To refer to the most ancient history of Stonehenge, critics must for their all-knowing purposes be in every one of the rings. They speak as if they had been, anyway. Surely critics were present when the first ditch was dug and the bank heaved up to contain the cattle; without any doubt they expressed an opinion of the original shape, extent, and digging techniques. Critics have long since rummaged in the burial-holes, and interpreted the beads and bones, the pot-fragments and weapon-parts. If in my metaphor the critics stand round the poet in an innermost ring, once upon a time they stood, and remember standing, in an older and outer ring. Critics remember and can judge the workmanship of every deep-based column, every mortised lintel; critics are quick to note a deviation from the master plan that was four thousand years in the carrying-out; critics always knew the temple's one purpose, which was to be ready for sunrise on Midsummer Day once every year. The critic is culture's conscience and memory and most severe instructor, because his perspective is long and his authority absolute, being simply truth. His surrounding presence and his fierce illumination is first acknowledged and most feared of them all. To the poet the other ringing presences bring nourishment, furnishing, praise, or attention. The critic is judgment.

Critics make new concepts, because in their long perspective they can see relationships hitherto overlooked. Stanley Edgar Hyman nominates Kenneth Burke's *Attitudes Toward History* as the outstanding book in criticism, of the last thirty years, for giving us the concept of symbolic action. (Critics, I might say, do not by nature nominate one another's books for honors.) This is a concept in which literary forms are attitudes toward experience. Literary works in the known forms become actions, for reader as well as writer. Despite the symbolic nature of these actions, they are as real and significant as any other. Therefore a poem is an action. Once this concept has been understood, it is never again possible to read poetry as one did before. Yeats, more by intuition and because he was a mythmaker, arrived at much the same thing. The poet who adds this tremendous faith to his stature need never doubt the poem's right to life. But more often what we get from the best critics is the closest possible reading of a text, with the fullest possible exploration of its sources and meanings. "To bring the poet back to life—the great, the perennial, task of criticism," says Eliot.

The ordinary reader of poetry, and I am an ordinary reader of it except that by avocation and devotion I have read more year in and year out than necessary, has first instinctive reactions to a poem; but does not trust them. Learning to trust one's first flashing reception is the secret. Reading Ezra Pound for the first time, I assumed that I was bewildered, ignorant, and mostly undesirable in Pound's audience. It was not that I did not experience the Cathay poems, or the *Draft of Thirty Cantos*, but I did not have, for instance, Kenneth Burke's assurance that a poem is an action for the reader. I did hear Pound's insistent voice in its many guises, but I could not tell myself that. I assumed I was bewildered. Not much later, I read R. P. Blackmur's "Masks of Ezra Pound," published in 1933 in *Hound and Horn*; I bought current issues of that unique and admirable quarterly. Blackmur said, with vigor and completeness and assurance, all that had dimly moved in my mind, all that I had not trusted in myself. These thirty years later, reading that essay again, it seems as right, as forthright, as final, as judgment can be.

In the same way, I look again with astonished and renewed self-trust at his early essays on Cummings' language; Marianne Moore's method; at his several essays on Yeats; again at the early and valid "Examples of Wallace Stevens"; and at his still continuing evaluations of Eliot. Blackmur seems to me the great critic of our time, our first best workman at the perennial task of bringing the poet back to life by reading him with fullest intelligence. The body of his writing, which includes much more reading and more difficult reading, of Henry James, D. H.

Lawrence, Melville, and others, would be paralyzing in its universal comprehension, if it were not that he writes so well, so like an impulsive, rational, brimming monologue by an expert. It demands the closest attention, but it can be read again, and will be read again. Blackmur speculates, too, and gives us reconsiderations and new conceptions, notably in his essay, " Language As Gesture "; his several essays on the art of criticism; and his important 1950 essay, " The Lion and the Honeycomb," which begins with the businesslike and infinitely promising sentence, " This paper proposes to examine into a certain section of the scholarship and criticism of poetry, and further proposes a possibility of expansion or growth for it."

What Blackmur does, we know is also done in exciting interaction by I. A. Richards, John Crowe Ransom, and T. S. Eliot; by principled independents like Louise Bogan, and Conrad Aiken, whose collected book reviews are basic reference; and by the best university essayists like Mark Van Doren, Cleanth Brooks, and Allen Tate—none of whom, in fact, would accept these categories. But all stand in those interwoven and everwatching rings in the new Stonehenge, where the poet imagines he is alone, but can never be alone.

VI

Crouched there on the sandstone altar, over his Stonehenge iii portable typewriter, or yellow copy paper, the poet might seem a flash-lighted, peered-upon, public event, as important as a fire or car-wreck. He is not yet a public event, and he does not know he is being watched; he is lonely, wretchedly happy, he rages in words, he changes the world. But no one knows. Except that he shows the poem to his teacher in school the next day, and she knows the world is changed, or could be changed. Teachers do not know everything, but sometimes some of them know when they are seeing the world change. Sometimes the crouching poet has one of those teachers.

Because of this one or that one, in the seventh or the ninth grade, he gets on his feet. In high school, in college, it goes to his head, and luck or his chromosomes, or one of the other gods, crosses him with his last teacher. What is in his head is what will make him a poet, and the good teacher is the one who notices and makes living-room for the shape of his head.

But more teachers teach poetry than teach poets. Whatever our huddled bard was doing at his desk, if his name was Scott, or Longfellow, or Burns—or if it was Wystan Auden, Wallace Stevens, or Anne Ridler—teachers would make more of it to more readers than ever the poet most wildly dreamed. Some of them would do it wildly, and wash it down with emotion. Some dutifully, in the misery of drill, would chalk the standard metrical forms on the blackboard, and scan the lines of a poem. But more than any census can report, there are teachers who transmit poem and poetry. One knows they renew poetry year after year, because of a light that comes into faces of their former students as they speak of " the course they'll never forget." The name of the teacher may be famous, and more likely not, but the name does not matter; there are great teachers, faithful and expert and sworn, of both kinds. To see that lighted face at its best, a shining of gratitude, personal devotion, and lasting assurance, one may meet a former student of Mark Van Doren's. His extraordinary lectures on Don Quixote, in his recent book, *The Happy Critic*, or his paper on the poetry of Thomas Hardy, give others some idea of the delighted knowledge he imparts. And he produces teachers of poetry; there is no end to it.

I have in my head a landmark map of the colleges and universities of this country, each campus starred with the name of a poet who teaches poetry there. The universities are the real foundational patrons of poetry. They employ poets and cherish them and let them talk; the other foundations merely give away money. New England bounds and abounds with poets: Rolfe Humphries at Amherst, Richard Eberhart at Dartmouth, May Sarton and David Ferry at Wellesley, Richard Wilbur at Wesleyan; Peter Viereck at Smith and Samuel French Morse at Mount Holyoke; Robert Penn Warren at Yale and Robert Lowell at Boston University, or lately so; William Jay Smith at Williams; and round about the nation, John Logan at Notre Dame, Howard Nemerov at Bennington, Philip Booth at Syracuse, Elder Olson at Chicago, Randall Jarrell at North Carolina, Yvor Winters at Stanford, Theodore Roethke at Washington, Theodore Weiss at Bard, Helen Bevington at Duke, Richmond Lattimore at Bryn Mawr, Donald Hall at Michigan— it would make a rich address-book for a cross-country tour.

That any of them is academic, in the very worst sense of that word, or live in ivory towers, in the most ridiculous sense of that word, is flatly untrue. Each in his official life is probably the least academized, the least towered, member of the university faculty. The best thing about the literary-educational-social phenomenon of poet on the university faculty is that he is honored for being himself, a free-flying bird in a natural, worldly cage. It is the historians, the language professors, the chemists, who are caged, care-ridden, and committeed nearly to death. The university poets are steady writers and frequent publishers, having the ideal situation for it. They teach either the writing, the history, or the evaluation of poetry, and thus exert prolonged and out-reaching influence. They review and discuss current poetry in the quarterlies, and in the largest newspapers and magazines. They are free to make public appearances, reading their poetry to audiences anywhere; to judge national poetry competitions; to help edit poetry magazines; and always and in the grand total, they are the hard core of the best audience for poetry. Professionalism, unquenchable appetite, or the juices of jealousy which in poets work very freely, make them the most ready and most constant readers of everything about poetry.

All these teachers of poetry, at every level, are better furnished with books and other materials than ever before. As textbooks, they have a range of anthologies, critical introductions to poetry as a subject, recordings by poets and other readers, and widely available magazine and newspaper material. The prime importance of poetry is assumed by the school and college systems, and abundantly supported by textbook publishers. Contemporary poetry has been taught by official consent and the teachers' knowledge for about thirty years now, which means that the beginnings were few and bold. But now there are several teacher-generations whose own school experience included modern poetry, and who know where to find it for classroom use—in paperback collections, in recordings, and so on. If the poet could see among his surroundings the ring of teachers, he might well feel crowded. But their direction is from him to students; they illuminate him not for his benefit but for the increase of his audience. He owes them more than gratitude. He owes them his life.

VII

One more ring, standing very close to the poet at work, might indeed jostle him, and seem to want to look over his shoulder while he writes, and to ask him to be a demonstrator of poetic composition, not one hard-breathing poet alone in a room with the English language. This watcher collects and studies the poet's very pages, the sheet after sheet on which he slowly forms his lines, and urges the poem into its right shape. This examiner of discarded work sheets re-enacts, as closely as he can, what the poet thought while he wrote—at the very instant, in the very setting down of the word. He cannot know all the poet thought and did not put on paper, but he can see in words written and crossed out, in lines roughly drafted and little by little smoothed and hardened, some tangible clues to what went on. He can reconstruct by intuitive guessing what the poet wanted to say, can feel the dulling and the firing of imagination. And he has the historical advantage over the poet of knowing beforehand how the poem did come out. He has his copy of the poem the way it now appears in books, the poem the poet hammered and scraped at in the rough, so doggedly making such difficult alterations that to the watcher seem so obviously, so easily, the changes that must be made. This new kind of scrutinizer, this double-ganger, this vicarious participator in the very pencil-work, is impelled to come as close as is physically and psychically possible to being the poet. Later he writes an account of the long step-by-step process he thinks the poet went through. The justification for this inside or almost-inside view is that nonwriters can learn from it how the poet's mind works. It is like taping electrodes to the skull, to listen to the brain's impulses. Either it is the most ruthless invasion of mind yet attempted, or it is the most daring exploration of the mysteries of literary creation. At very best—that is, even with much-scribbled-over work sheets for tangible evidence—it is an incomplete revelation. But this curiosity about the fits and starts, the rumblings and the lion's leap,

that go on in the poet's mind, is a recent thing. I think the
unspoken motive is an utterly innocent admiration for the
unknown and unimaginable freedom of the poet's mind, a
hunger for the supreme excitement of the artist's ultimate experience. I resent it, too. The poet's maunderings, wanderings, and
fireworks in his subconscious and unconscious ought to be in-
violable privacies. But the poet is doomed to ritual. When in
my metaphor the sun rises on Midsummer Day, and the blazing
light falls as the priests planned it, on the poet hunched there
over his notebooks, the listeners and the watchers partake of the
blood sacrifice. My metaphor is only a reminding device, though;
the bleeding is not mortal. Poets like to bleed.

Reproductions of poets' work sheets have been appearing in
textbooks on the understanding of poetry in recent years. Successive drafts are shown with as much realism as typography can
manage—the cancellations, the alternate wordings, the unsuc-
cessful early lines. Inch by inch a stanza grows, the poem grows,
and we are allowed this close-up, this naked documentation. The
supposition seems to be that if we share the struggle of evolve-
ment, we more fully comprehend the poem. I am not convinced.
I think it is like poking around a painter's studio when he is not
there, and seeing what he mixes for his famous colors, how dirty
he lets his brushes be, or what variety of sizes of brushes he has.
Oil-painting is a messy and tedious thing, and a good analogy
for writing poems; a poet's work sheets are tedious, and his
workshop messy. The dominant and unsuspected fact is that
so much drudgery went into the making. Such clumsiness, such
mumbling—then the stroke!

One of the great collections of poets' notebooks and work
sheets is at the University of Buffalo, in the Lockwood Library,
made by the late Charles Abbott. Massive accumulators of rich

raw materials know, I hope for his sake, that intention can be immortality. His intention was that poets and critics and teachers should penetrate the mystery of poetic composition. An exciting early result was Donald Stauffer's reactivation of R. P. Blackmur's poem, "Missa Vocis." In an essay called "Genesis, or the Poet As Maker," in a book Charles Abbott edited, called *Poets At Work*, Stauffer prints first the finished poem. He admires in much detail the apparently controlled total structure. Then he shows us six successive versions, in the poet's hand, and we learn after the most sensitive, informed, and obedient attention to the poem's growth, that " chance flowers into choice." We see that the way to write a poem is to write a poem. It begins cold and clumsy, warms itself, and marvelously, openly, to the astonishment of no one as much as the poet himself, comes alive in its own generative heat. Stauffer concludes that "the progress of the artist in creation is always toward greater purity, intensity, and unity," that the close examination of work sheets proves that it is the cumulative effect of small changes, of happy contrivings, of careful tending, that makes the poem the poem it meant to be.

Charles Abbott used to lecture on certain sets of work sheets in his collection. No one perhaps could or should follow the geologic growth of Dylan Thomas's " Hunchback In the Park," but the manuscript is available. It was a surprise to me that Kenneth Fearing tried out so many versions of an apparently effortless, colloquial New-York-talk piece. The Abbott collection shows almost endless testings of casual idiom, all trying to say the same thing, none quite right to Kenneth Fearing's ear. The reading and re-reading is tedious and very sobering, until at last the perfectly plain phrase comes. This tediousness was even more oppressive, and frustration greater, when Abbott presented

Stephen Spender's gropings for the now inevitable lines of
"Landscape Near an Aerodrome." Spender's early notebooks are
in the University of Buffalo collection. How could he write a
run of such beautiful lines, and then so blindly not say what he
must say next? Stephen Spender, of course, had not yet seen
the famous poem in the anthologies of a decade later. But it
is a shocking first lesson to beginning poets that their heroes have
hands of clay more usually than the vision of gods, and that
writing poetry is labor upon blind stubborn labor. There is a
set of work sheets in this same library that shows Richard
Wilbur's lively start at his poem, "The Juggler." Before the
juggler begins to perform—and such airy performance at a
country fair called eternity is the best of a Wilbur poem—the
poet somehow came of several minds about the juggler's costume.
He spent precious lines and energy on its checkerings, colors,
till as the manuscript shows, he resorted to prose description
of the simple event itself, before he could outlaw gravity, get
the flashing balls into the air, and the poem going. The poem
is a triumph, and it is a poem about triumph.

What these spyings show, as they occur in the inner precinct
of the temple, where the poet works surrounded and illuminated
by poets, biographies, editors, critics, teachers, and readers—these
peerings and pokings—is how terribly poetry is cared for. I mean
the uncontrollable curiosity, the powerful necessity of hunger
and wonder about poetry, as beauty and terror draw us. These
scrutinizers of the-poem-in-process are the really first readers;
they read it before the poet reads it. They carry the report,
plucked out of danger, back to the ordinary reader, to the teacher,
further back to the critic and editor, and all the way back to
the biographer. John Milton's ode, "At a Solemn Musick,"
has a line for which he chose the fifth of seven possibilities

from his drafts. " To live and sing with him in *ever-endless, ever-glorious, uneclipsed, where day swells without night, in endless morne of light, in cloudless birth, in never parting light,*" became finally, " To live and sing with him in endless morn of light." Robert Frost wrote, " My little *mare* must think it queer," and " Between the *forest and the* lake," and improved both lines in revision. Housman's alternatives are known, which would displease him; and Allen Tate's decade-long revision of his " Ode to the Confederate Dead " is a famous documented example in our time of the public claim and interest in such matters. A wondering! but no wonder.

To review the concentric assembly I have summoned up in this metaphor of Stonehenge, in which all eyes fix the poet, is to confirm M. L. Rosenthal's idea that of all figures in 20th-century public life, the poet is the hero who can lead us to salvation. The poet seeks life with honor, for himself and us. Robinson recorded failures in the search; Pound recounts a bitter defeat and exile; Yeats more than any is the hero as poet, defies and despises politics and money-making, and magnificently completes his image of himself as artist; Stevens hides himself for art's sake, in art, the only salvation, satisfaction, and way of life. Our eyes are on the poet as hero.

May Sarton

This is the School of Babylon
And at its hands we learn
To walk into the furnaces
And whistle as we burn.

Thomas Blackburn

The School
of
Babylon

I MUST WARN YOU AT ONCE that I am not a critic, except of my own work, but perhaps I should not offer this fact as an apology for surely the great poet-critics of our time—Yeats, Valéry, Eliot—have used what has been sometimes taken as dispassionate criticism of others as a means of orienting themselves and of grounding their own work in an aesthetic. Perhaps criticism from poets is always self-criticism.

I should like to reconsider and shape once more some tentative answers to questions I have been asking myself for twenty-five years, questions about tension and equilibrium within the writing of poetry and within the poet's life. It is, in fact, just twenty-five years since my first book of poems appeared, and I am now close to the half-century myself, a good moment for such meditations.

Eugen Herrigel in a small but explosive book, *Zen in the Art of Archery*, speaks of the aim of the Zen masters as not "the ability of the sportsman, which can be controlled, more or less,

27

by bodily exercises, but an ability whose origin is to be sought in spiritual exercises and whose aim consists in hitting a spiritual goal, so that fundamentally the marksman aims at himself and may even succeed in hitting himself." So let me draw my bow and point the arrow inward . . .

I have an idea that somewhere in his forties the poet reaches a turning point, at which he either becomes a more public or a more private person, that he has a choice, and on that choice depends the kind of work he will produce, as well as the kind of life he will live. In the dialogue between the world and himself, he fights to preserve the innocence and the intensity without which art cannot exist. And it is just when he is in his forties that the pressures to lecture, to review other men's books, and to be a public person begin to assert themselves. My theme is tension in equilibrium, that dangerous tension, that perilous equilibrium which exist in every great poem, and in the life of every poet; and I have just touched on one of the permanent tensions, that between the public and the private person, the poet who lectures and the poet who writes the poems: they are opposite poles. Each of us seeks out his own solution to this never-solved problem. Mine has been, in the last three years, to spend five months at least of every year in a village in New Hampshire. There I can study the ferocity of nature and realize (it is consoling in a way) that beside it the ferocity of poets and the critics of poets is child's play. But I suspect, nevertheless, that the tension between the public and private self is not an unfruitful one. One of the fascinations of Yeats' growth is that his assaults on the world, as a founder of the Abbey Theatre, and later as a senator, helped him to forge his style. Without the fierce tension between what he called "The Mask and the Self," would he have hammered out the iron of his later style? Who knows?

Tension . . . my Webster defines it in several ways. Here are three which I can appropriate: 1) A strained condition of relations, as between nations. 2) A device to produce a desired tension or pull, as in a loom. 3) *Elec.*: The quality in consequence of which an electric charge tends to discharge itself.

As I pondered these provocative definitions, I jotted down some of the tensions I experience in the process of writing a poem, tensions which discharge a load of experience in a most beneficent and exciting way when the piece of weaving on the loom turns out to be a real poem:

1) The tension between past and present,
2) between idea and image,
3) between music and meaning,
4) between particular and universal,
5) between creator and critic,
6) between silence and words.

Parallel with them are the tensions within daily life:

1) between the living and the dead,
2) between the public and the private person,
3) between art and life.

Once I had noted down these apparently organized but actually haphazard ideas, I took refuge at once in the equilibrium and organization of a poem, Thomas Blackburn's "The School of Babylon," from which I have borrowed the title of this essay. (The relief it was to rest in this "momentary stay against confusion"!) I might tell you that the epigraph of Blackburn's poem is from Daniel, "Men loose walking in the midst of fire" (3:25). This is the second and final stanza:

Although a wine-glass or a cup
Can hold as little of the sea
As you and I of our own selves,
Pin-pointed by mortality,
We still, that something of the whole,
May quicken in the finite part,
Must labour for a deeper breath
And greater tension of the heart.
Out of their windy distances
The further energies draw near
And kindling in our tongues and hands
Increase the glory and the fear.
But still as the unspoken word
Swings slowly downward into speech
And in becoming us reveals
Another word beyond our reach,
We praise the School of Babylon,
For where else could we learn
To walk into the furnaces
And whistle as we burn?

Of course, one of the springs of poetry is our strained relations with our own immediate past, the warring nations within the self; then the poem itself becomes a device by means of which this electric charge discharges itself. And one of the springs of poetry is joy—joy and grief as opposed to happiness and depression; the difference in in*tens*ity between the former and the latter is my point. In a formal sense, each poem also discharges and balances the tension between the whole past of poetic invention and itself; each new poem is partly propelled by the formal energies of all the poems that have preceded it in the history of literature. Those poets who wish to affirm their freedom from the past by pretending that all old forms are dead, deny themselves this fruitful tension. Their poems are intended to be wholly " present," but we experience the present as a kind of equilibrium between past and future, and there is only tension, no balance between present and future. Such poems, like the children of *Brave New World*, are test-tube poems. I think that the answer may be in the distance in time between the points of tension: we have to move back more than one generation to find the fruitful polarity. Valéry makes this clear in his unexpected praise of Victor Hugo (the poet's Hugo as against the public's Hugo) for going back to the then unfashionable sixteenth-century French poets for some of his forms. So Hugo remains a source in a way that Vigny, de Musset, Lamartine do not.

" The poetic player," as Valéry puts it in another context, " can choose his game: some prefer roulette, others chess." If you are a chess player, what you are looking for is a new opening, a new device by which you may win within the old rules; a means of taking your opponent by surprise. The dynamics of form have to do with our initimate relation with the past, and our natural instinct for what we can use for a particular poem, the form that can best become a vehicle for its electric current, the tension between the whole rich past and this poem *now*. Like a pregnant woman who must suddenly have strawberries, I once found myself going back to Herbert for the form of a poem which created an equilibrium for me (in this case a permanent one) out of the excruciating tensions set up by my mother's death from cancer. The poem itself I could only write four years later; I could write it partly because I had found in George Herbert a viable structure.

Sometimes the polarity expresses itself, not through metrics, but by means of an echo. Eliot has often used this device, in the earlier poems for purposes of irony, in the later ones as a

way of condensing time. How effective it can be, Yeats proved
in " A Bronze Head," when suddenly he allows Herbert and
the particular reverberations Herbert brings with him to act as
catharsis for his revaluation of Maud Gonne. I need not remind
you of the climax of Herbert's " The Collar ":

> But as I rav'd and grew more fierce and wilde
> At every word,
> Me thought I heard one calling, *Child*!
> And I reply'd, *My Lord*.

Here is the third stanza of " A Bronze Head ":

> But even at the starting-post, all sleek and new,
> I saw the wildness in her and I thought
> A vision of terror that it must live through
> Had shattered her soul. Propinquity had brought
> Imagination to that pitch where it casts out
> All that is not itself: I had grown wild
> And wandered murmuring everywhere, 'My child, my child!'

And let us not forget that, as Valéry says, "Everyone knows
that to aim at not following or imitating someone is still in some
way to imitate him. The mirror reverses images." The poet
cannot escape from the tension between past and present even
when the tension is expressed by total rejection of the past.

He cannot do so any more than any one of us can escape
from our own individual past, for to do so is to murder a part
of ourselves. The tension between the living and the dead,
especially perhaps that between oneself and one's parents, after
their death, may become especially powerful in middle age.

John Holmes and Richard Eberhart have been overtly concerned in their poetry with finding and explaining the equilibrium between themselves and their parents. (Again we pull

the bow far back to loose the arrow). Eberhart can say it all
in three lines:

> And I stare, rich with gifts, alone,
>
> Feeling from the sea those terrene presences,
> My father's hands, my mother's eyes.

Yeats' father and grandfather are always there back of the poems,
and so too with Edwin Muir. I must regard my whole life as
an attempt to bring into focus and so be able fully to use the
rich gifts I was given by a scholar father and an artist mother,
each strong in his own right. I do not summon them, but they
are there, pivotal tensions. Everything must be tested and questioned against their innocence, their passion, and my whole life
a precarious balance between their two kinds of genius.

Let us return to poetry itself and the writing of poems. At
once I find myself rebelling against the act of criticism because
it must, if it is to explain anything at all, make an indivisible
act divisible and partial. In fact, it is possible that we recognize
the birth of a true poem as distinct from what Louise Bogan calls
"imitation poems" by this very state, a state in which a series
of complexes exist *together*, and find their way to equilibrium
without ever having been separated out into distinct functions
or threads. Idea and image, music and meaning, creation and
criticism, the particular and the universal, silence and utterance—
when we are ready to write a poem, all these separate modes
work together at the same time. "Poetry," as Valéry puts it,
"must extend over the whole being; it stimulates the muscular
organization by its rhythms, it frees or unleashes the verbal
faculties, ennobling their whole action, it regulates our depths,
for poetry aims to arouse or reproduce the unity and harmony
of the living person, an extraordinary unity that shows itself

when a man is possessed by an intense feeling that leaves none of his powers disengaged." Unfortunately the act of criticism imposes the necessity to disengage certain powers, and is therefore always in some sense, false.

A true poem does not begin with a feeling, however compelling, and of course we feel a great many things that never become poems. A poem emerges when a tension that *has been* something experienced, felt, seen, suddenly *releases* a kind of anxious stirring about of words and images; at this moment there is a mysterious shift of energy; the energy that was absorbed in experience itself, now becomes an energy of an entirely different kind, and all that matters is to solve the sort of puzzle, the sort of maze in which certain phrases, and a certain rhythm lie around like counters in a game of Scrabble. So a great grief may turn into a certain kind of imaginative energy and lift the sufferer right out of himself into the joys of creation.

Let me give you a ludicrous example which will serve as well as any to give you some idea as to how the process works. Some years ago, shortly after I moved into my New Hampshire house, I was given a magnificent Teddy bear as a Valentine and he has become one of the Lares, sits on a big desk in the little parlor and emits a muted bellow when you pick him up. One day I seemed to hear him singing a little song, a rhyme, and, once in my head, I could not get it out for a whole day. It goes

> Only, only,
> lonely, lonely,
> moanly, moanly,
> groanly, groanly.

True poems may make their appearance in just the way this rhyme did, and take over the day, interrupt whatever we may be doing, insist on making themselves heard, willy-nilly. For us, who are not Teddy bears, the music may be more subtle, though it may not (you remember Edith Sitwell's "Daisy and Lily, lazy and silly," no doubt?). In a true poem, this "musical stir" as Maritain calls it, this tension of a phrase asking to be musically resolved, is always accompanied by an image. The rhyme of the bear is not a poem for many reasons, and one is that the bear himself does not appear. If the bear-song could have incorporated bear himself, it might have become one. Everything in the psyche takes place for a reason. Why did something in me identify itself with the Teddy bear? No doubt I too was feeling lonely and moanly. If this state had been about to be translated into a poem, I would have had to enter the maze of bear, the puzzle of bear and find my way out of it, or rather *into* its center and heart. And I might have sat down to ask myself some questions.

Did the bear begin to sing for me because he suggests innocence, childhood, and also the whole unconscious animal world, the sensual world, of which at that time I felt deprived? And is the sensual world always there when we feel wholly ourselves? So that to be deprived of our animal self is in some way to be deprived also of its polarity, the angel self? The bear seems also to be consolation—he sings a lonely song because I feel lonely, and I am comforted by this image of childhood. Why is an image of childhood consoling to an adult?

But while I am asking myself these questions, the music the bear is chanting runs along all the time underneath, emerging now and then into an actual phrase, imposing upon me the metrical form the poem will take. And a high tension, a delightful inner humming is set up between the apparently innocuous rhyme, the image back of it, and my own response, both conscious and unconscious, to what is going on in my head.

There are points at which the arts, especially those of painting and poetry, bisect each other. Painters, too, think their way through, by means of images lifted out by a present shock of emotion, and polarizing the whole past. I want to steal here a fairly long excerpt from Ben Shahn's book *The Shape of Content.* He is analyzing the sources of a painting of his called "Allegory." The immediate seminal image was that of a fire in Chicago in which a colored man had lost his four children.

It seemed to me that the implications of this event transcended the immediate story; there was a universality about man's dread of fire, and his sufferings from fire. There was a universality in the pity which such disaster invokes. Even racial injustice, which had played its part in this event, had its overtones . . .

I now began to devise symbols of an almost abstract nature, to work in terms of such symbols. Then I rejected that approach too. For in the abstracting of an idea one may lose the very intimate humanity of it, and this deep and common tragedy was above all things human. I returned then to the small family contacts, to the familiar experiences of all of us, to the furniture, the clothes, the look of ordinary people, and on that level made my bid for universality and for the compassion that I hoped and believed the narrative would arouse.

Of all the symbols which I had begun or sought to develop, I retained only one in my illustrations—a highly formalized wreath of flames with which I crowned the plain shape of the house which had burned. . . .

The narrative of the fire had roused in me a chain of personal memories. There were two great fires in my own childhood, one only colorful, the other disastrous and unforgettable. Of the first, I remember only that the little Russian village in which my grandfather lived burned, and I was there. I remember the excitement, the flames breaking out everywhere, the lines of men passing buckets to and from the river which ran through the town, the mad-woman who had escaped from someone's house during the confusion, and whose face I saw, dead-white in all the reflected color.

The other fire left its mark upon me and all my family, and left its scars on my father's hands and face, for he had clambered up a drain-pipe and taken each of my brothers and sisters and me out of the house one by one, burning himself painfully in the process. Meanwhile our house and all our belongings were consumed, and my parents stricken beyond their power to recover.

Among my discarded symbols pertaining to the Hickman story there were a number of heads and bodies of beasts, besides several Harpies, Furies, and other symbolic semi-classical shapes and figures. Of one of these, a lion-like head, but still not a lion, I made many drawings, each drawing approaching more nearly some inner figure of primitive terror which I was seeking to capture. I was beginning to become most familiar with this beast-head. It was, you might say, under control. . . .

When at last I turned the lion-like beast into a painting, I felt able to imbue it with everything that I had ever felt about a fire. I incorporated the highly formalized flames from the Hickman story as a wreath about its head, and under its body I placed the four child figures which, to me, hold the sense of all the helpless and innocent.

The image that I sought to create was not one of *a* disaster; that somehow does not interest me. I wanted instead to create the emotional tone that surrounds disaster; you might call it inner disaster.

When I read these pages, I recognized the analogy with a poet's images and how he unearths them. For here, too, we may sometimes begin with an actual scene, witnessed, but it will only become material for poetry if it is able to magnetize to itself a part of the inner world as well, if it reverberates. There is some truth, I think, in the criticism of the poets called "academic" (I fear I am one of them!) for being overconcerned with the decorative aspects of language. A poem does not move us deeply, I believe, unless the central image is capable of stirring us below the level of consciousness, is, in fact, an archetype. For the metaphor holds the explosive power of the poem. This explosion may take place on the surface of the mind, in which case it gives a moment's pleasure, or it may take place in the mysterious inner recesses of being, in which case the poem may well do what Rilke asks of art at the end of his sonnet on the "Archaic Torso of Apollo":

> Here there is nothing that does not see you:
> You must change your life.

The most viable metaphor contains the greatest possible number of tensions and at the same time releases them. And we are changed by it not because we have been told about something, but because a whole series of inner actions have been set in motion by it and at the same time to some extent resolved. Something has been changed at the center of consciousness, forever.

The surface image is a temptation to every poet; for if he is a poet at all, he is apt to think in images and every abstract idea comes to him immediately translated into a concrete exemplar. But every time he writes a real poem, he will find himself polarized in a tension so complex and painful that it forces him to deepen and explore below the surface. It is the complex charge of the image in Richard Wilbur's "The Grave" that gives this poem its power . . . at first a private dream, the return in dream of the dog he had loved as a boy and did not have the courage to bury when it died; this image explodes by the end of the poem. Through it, Wilbur is able to make a cool deep incision into all our guilt about the dead, and to let some of the poison out. The poem in this instance is an act of grace.

Tension between idea and image has to do with the depth and complexity of the image; if it is an inspired image, i. e., one that comes from deep enough below the surface, it may very probably change the original idea, for the image is all the time pointing the way to what we really mean, and not what we thought we meant. In this sense the image is ethical. As Bachelard, the French psychologist who has devoted himself to examining metaphor, says: " we are here at a center where ideas dream and where images think."

" The Combat " by Edwin Muir throws us a naked metaphor so powerful that I have never recovered from my first reading of it, and to re-read it is merely to resume aloud, the uninterrupted reverberations that it set up.

> It was not meant for human eyes,
> That combat on the shabby patch
> Of clods and trampled turf that lies
> Somewhere beneath the sodden skies
> For eye of toad or adder to catch.

> And having seen it I accuse
> The crested animal in his pride,
> Arrayed in all the royal hues
> Which hide the claws he well can use
> To tear the heart out of the side.

> Body of leopard, eagle's head
> And whetted beak, and lion's mane,
> And frost-grey hedge of feathers spread
> Behind—he seemed of all things bred.
> I shall not see his like again.

As for his enemy, there came in
A soft round beast as brown as clay;
All rent and patched his wretched skin;
A battered bag he might have been,
Some old used thing to throw away.

Yet he awaited face to face
The furious beast and the swift attack.
Soon over and done. That was no place
Or time for chivalry or for grace.
The fury had him on his back.

And two small paws like hands flew out
To right and left as the trees stood by.
One would have said beyond a doubt
This was the very end of the bout,
But that the creature would not die.

For ere the death-stroke he was gone,
Writhed, whirled, huddled into his den,
Safe somehow there. The fight was done,
And he had lost who had all but won.
But oh his deadly fury then.

A while the place lay blank, forlorn,
Drowsing as in relief from pain.
The cricket chirped, the grating thorn
Stirred, and a little sound was born.
The champions took their posts again.

And all began. The stealthy paw
Slashed out and in. Could nothing save
These rags and tatters from the claw?
Nothing. And yet I never saw
A beast so helpless and so brave.

And now, while the trees stand watching, still
The unequal battle rages there.

> The killing beast that cannot kill
> Swells and swells in his fury till
> You'd almost think it was despair.

There, I hope you will agree, is an image in poetry that can be set beside Ben Shahn's lion-head of fire.

Just as we "must labour for a deeper breath and greater tension of the heart" when we come to use or discard the metaphors that pass through the waking mind when a poem is in process, so we must labour too, to deepen, and even sometimes roughen, the too facile music that floats about on the surface of consciousness. Yeats spent a lifetime working toward the tone, the rhythm, the tune that would express the rigor and complexity of what he had to say as he moved away from the superficial singing of the Lake Isle toward the resinous speech of the Last Poems. In a letter of 1916, he is already worrying this problem: "I separate the rhythmical and the abstract. They are brothers, but one is Abel and one is Cain. In poetry they are not confused for we know that poetry is rhythm, but in music-hall verses we find an abstract cadence, which is vulgar because it is apart from imitation. This cadence is a mechanism, it never suggests a voice shaken with joy or sorrow as poetical rhythm does. It is but the noise of a machine and not the coming and going of the breath."

Poetry finds its perilous equilibrium somewhere between music and speech, and each poet as he comes along has to breathe his own breath, find his own intervals that will make it "sound right" for him. How various the solutions may be can be apprehended if we juxtapose Robert Frost and Paul Valéry! One reason I have found myself going back to Herbert is to try to catch his intervals, the swing of his pendulum between music and meaning, between music and speech . . . we are not floated down the poem like paper boats; we are absorbed into it by strange little pauses and irregularities of breathing, as if indeed a voice were speaking aloud to us now:

> Ah, my deare angrie Lord,
> Since thou dost love, yet strike;
> Cast down, yet help afford;
> Sure I will do the like.
>
> I will complain, yet praise;
> I will bewail, approve:
> And all my soure-sweet dayes
> I will lament, and love.

Even when he uses this simplest of all forms, you see, the cadence is highly individual, his own voice.

Once again—it is, after all, my theme—what becomes clear is that facility (lack of tension) is the enemy of poetry. The very poverty of rhyme in the English language gives us an advantage, I sometimes think, over the French poet, crowded in, as by a flock of pigeons, by the hundreds of rhyming words. Rhyme in English is a hard master. The obstacles that it raises in the current of our thought slow us down, make us think, and of course also sometimes (there is a saving grace!) bring us the lucky chance that may enrich meaning in unexpected ways.

> I could give all to Time except—except
> What I myself have held.

says Mr. Frost. Might one not speak in somewhat the same terms of the struggle within the writing of each poem? A great deal has to be given up, so that when we come to the end, we do say, "And what I would not part with, I have kept." We have come through some real dangers and taken some real risks. The music, the images, and the propulsive idea, all these make

intricate and sometimes apparently opposite demands. From the
tensions between them, when they arrive at an equilibrium,
poised on all the dangers, like a bird in the air, the poem soars.
As Henry Adams says at the end of *Mont St. Michel and
Chartres*, " The equilibrium is visibly delicate beyond the line of
safety; danger lurks in every stone."

I fear I have been rather solemn about what the French
troubadours knew as the " gai scavoir." But I hope it goes without saying that, just as the joy of playing tennis for the player
is the mastery of the continual stress of the game, and if it were
easier to play, it would not be half as much fun, so the poet
of course is never happier, nor more wholly himself, than when
he is engaged in the play of writing a poem, in making the
puzzle " come out right." And the longer he can tease it along,
the happier he is, if he is a poet like Valéry. Of course there
is the final danger of crossing the intangible frontier beyond
which a poem is damaged by more manipulation . . . it may
suddenly go dead like the mouse which the cat has played with.
When is a poem finished?

The answer is, I think, when all the tensions it has posited
are perfectly equilibrated, when the change of a single syllable
would so affect the structure that the poem would fall like a
house of cards under the shift. But Valéry's answer to when a
poem is finished would be, " never." Valéry was that rarest of
poets—one for whom the ultimate release was in the artifice itself
(he did not *want* to finish), as against Yeats for whom the release
was in equilibrating tensions *back* of the poem *by means* of it.
Yeats could say, " They and their sort alone earn contemplation,
for it is only when the intellect has wrought the whole of life
to drama, to crisis, that we may live for contemplation and yet
keep our intensity." Valéry could say, " My poem ' Le Cimetière

Marin ' began in me by a rhythm, that of a French line . . . of ten syllables, divided into four and six. I had as yet no idea with which to fill this form. Gradually a few hovering words settled in it, little by little determining the subject . . ." I need not remind you, I am sure, that this turned into one of the few great metaphysical poems written in our time. It is clear that we do not exactly choose our poems; our poems choose us.

Poems may never be finished if one is Valéry, but essays must come to an end. It was my intention when I began to think about *The School of Babylon* to avoid using any poem of my own as illustration. But it now seems to me that the analysis of someone else's poem, one of those by John Holmes, Richard Eberhart, Richard Wilbur or Randall Jarrell which would have been appropriate, could be an act of hubris. For who am I to describe the process by which any of them came into being? I can only speak with authority about process in relation to my own work.

Probably Thomas Blackburn's poem moves me as it does because it articulates almost every element that goes into the writing of poetry and the poet's life as I see them. The refrain of the first stanza, the one I did not quote goes:

> This is the School of Babylon
> And at its hands we learn
> To walk into the furnaces
> And whistle as we burn.

Here we find Yeats' vision and Valéry's fused. We must be " men loose walking in the midst of fire," and men or women who find it possible to whistle as they burn. The writing of poetry is the whistling. But if we did not dare walk into the furnaces, there would be no occasion for whistling. Whistling in the dark is another matter!

We go to school to a complex, demanding art so that we may learn a device for discharging tensions and apprehensions which we might not otherwise have strength to bear, and which as it is, become simply transposable *energy*. So grief itself is transposed into a curious joy.

I shall close with a poem of mine called "Lifting Stone." The image came to me through a painting by Katharine Sturgis, a semiabstract water color of a piece of granite being lifted out of a quarry. I saw the painting first more than ten years ago, but could not afford to buy it. Still, it haunted me. And when it reappeared, in a show, still unsold, years after my first meeting with it, I felt this was a sign. I had better buy it and live with it and understand *why* I was haunted.

The image was evidently one of those complex ones which had something to reveal if I could explore it down deep enough, explore it by making a poem out of it. Quarries give us to dream. I sensed slowly that one of the reasons why is the fact that we dig down deep into the earth to bring up the stones that will eventually soar in the cathedrals—as we dig down to the subconscious matrix to bring up the images that fertilize the imagination. No height without depth.

But there was another element in the painting, the equilibrium of the pulley itself, lifting this immense stone pillar on a steel thread, as if the stone were a mere feather. Here tension could be seen equilibrated in the most delicate possible way. Thirdly, in Katharine Sturgis' painting, the whole composition centered in the abstract figure of a man, standing way down deep inside, directing the operation. I had at the time, been reading Herrigel. Let us go back to him for a moment now. Herrigel worked for five years with a Zen master in Japan before he even began to learn the self-abstraction and the technical

skill to understand the art of the archer. Sometime in the fifth
year he tells us,

> One day the Master cried out the moment my shot was
> loosed: "It is there! Bow down to the goal!" Later, when I
> glanced towards the target—unfortunately I couldn't help my-
> self—I saw that the arrow had only grazed the edge. "That
> was a right shot," said the Master decisively, "and so it must
> begin. But enough for today, otherwise you will take special
> pains with the next shot, and spoil the good beginning." . . .
> During those weeks and months I passed through the
> hardest schooling of my life, and though the discipline was
> not always easy for me to accept, I gradually came to see how
> much I was indebted to it. It destroyed the last traces of any
> preoccupation with myself and the fluctuations of my mood.
> "Do you now understand," the Master asked me one day after
> a particularly good shot, "what I mean by 'It shoots,' 'It
> hits'?"
> "I'm afraid I don't understand anything more at all," I
> answered," even the simplest things have got into a muddle.
> Is it 'I' who draws the bow, or is it the bow that draws me
> into the state of highest tension? Do 'I' hit the goal, or does
> the goal hit me? Is 'It' spiritual when seen with the eyes of
> the body, and corporeal when seen by the eyes of the spirit—
> or both or neither? Bow, arrow, goal and ego, all melt into one
> another, so that I can no longer separate them. And even the
> need to separate has gone. For as soon as I take the bow and
> shoot, everything becomes clear and straightforward and
> ridiculously simple . . ."
> "Now at last," the Master broke in, "the bowstring has
> cut right through you."

What held me here, as it did in Katharine Sturgis' painting
was once more that at the point of highest tension, lies also
the point of supreme release. In the end what is most difficult
becomes most easy, what was heaviest to lift becomes light as

air . . . and this happens, of course, when we are not thinking of ourselves at all, but have become instruments of an art or craft. At such a time it may be possible for a master like Frost in the art of poetry to sit down after a long night's work on something else and set down " Stopping by Woods on a Snowy Evening," without a pause, as a Japanese painter in one stroke paints a piece of bamboo and it is " right."

Lifting Stone

This is an ancient scene: we stand and stare
As hills are excavated and then lifted;
Swung on the cable's perpendicular,
The load is pivotal to earth and air,
A feather-balance, and so delicate
The stone floats up as if it had no weight.

Below, a solitary figure stands
To gentle the long bundle from its bed;
Athens and Troy are leaning from his hands;
The Roman arch, then perilous Chartres ascends
Out of the empty spacious world where he
Nudges rich burdens toward history.

Who with his own machineries of skill
Has not dreamed often of this very place?
Painter and poet lift the buried hill
To build a pyramid or clean bright wall,
And the great spires that sleep in this quarry
Are excavated toward the clouds they marry.

What soars is always buried deep for ages,
Gently explored in the hill's dark mind,
Prized, hewn in slow thoughtful stages,
Then floated on these airy equipages,
Watched by a figure standing there alone
Whose work, humble and hard, is lifting stone.

Richard Eberhart

Will and
Psyche
in Poetry

I WISH TO EXAMINE THE RELA-
tion of Will and Psyche to poetry.

I conceive these terms as op-
posite poles of a modern dichotomy, but they may lie at the
root of the mind itself and go back to the beginning of thought.
I choose them because they have impinged upon my consciousness for years. It would be possible to attempt a reduction of
the reality of poetry under a multiple aegis, or to accept a uni-
tarian principle. However, it is natural to me to think in terms
of dualism; if it is too neat to cast everything into either black
or white, it is also orderly, and forces an arbitrary, though not
conclusive, order on what is discovered.

The presumption of poetic criticism is intellectual authority.
By thinking about poetry one can make certain determinations.
This is the play of the mind, a pleasurable exercise. I do not
say that truth is to be found, nor that what authority one comes
by is not itself subject to the sway of time. What I affirm is
the relativity of truth within absolute limits and the normalcy
of a dichotomous look at poetry. There is a certain modesty

in my approach. One does not wish absolutism, but a relative sagacity. After reading criticism for thirty years, it is necessary to wipe the slate clean, and speak freely with all one's impurities upon one. There is a vast body of historical poetry, to which accretions are always being made. It may be of interest to look at certain types of poetry, certain poems under an arbitrary canon. I shall study poetry from the creative, or poet's, point of view rather than from the presumptions of a reader who is not a poet and has no desire to write poetry. Maybe the line between creative reading and creative writing is thin. Maybe the approach of a dualism here is mythical. In any case, my remarks shall be, I hope, exploratory rather than dogmatic.

In thinking of Will and Psyche a battery of descriptive terms comes at once to mind. Will is of the body; Psyche, or Soul, is of or beyond the mind. Will is flesh; Psyche spirit: Will is active; Psyche passive. Will makes something happen, or wishes to make something happen; Psyche makes nothing happen. Will is impure; Psyche is pure. Will represents struggle and effort; Psyche represents an uncontaminated grace. Will is the body of this world; Psyche is the elusive, passive, imaginative quality of or toward another. Will is interested; Psyche is disinterested. Will goes back to some basic power in the cell, an animal exercise. The cell has an excess of energy over its power to maintain itself.

Psyche is at once mysterious and eludes the simplest opposition to what I have just said. I suppose it depends upon a cellular structure for none of us living can feel what it is to be dead and only by imagination, by intuitive leaps, can we dream beyond death. Here many ideas about Psyche appear. If one equates it with soul, then we may say it is the soul; but nobody knows what the soul is. I have touched my flesh for years trying to find my soul. I have still not seen it. But there are ancient, persistent ideas about the soul. There is, for instance, the Platonic world soul, envisaged as a vast amorphous cloud hanging in the heavens. When we are born a portion of the world soul is attached to our body, where it lives while we live; when we die, it ascends, or departs, depicted in old paintings always upwards, back to the mother lode or static whole of the world soul. There are all the variations of Eastern philosophy, thought, and religion about the soul and the afterlife. However, to write the last few sentences I must be corporeal; it is easy to insist upon this! Therefore, by reason we may say that we do not know whether we have a soul, but without an undue amount of sympathetic projection we may assume that we have a soul, a Psyche, somewhere about us.

In a short space and time the easy absolutes mentioned above have broken open into what may be seen at once to verge upon massive speculations. This is part of the fascination of the problem. We start by saying that Will and Psyche enforce a real dichotomy, but almost at once it is seen that these terms exfoliate and proliferate; that there may, maybe must, be some Psyche in Will, for how could it be so base a thrust as by strong nature not to possess some qualities of the divine? And how could Psyche be so pure as not to possess some qualities of base human nature? They may not be white and black as we suppose. Indeed, it may be that some of the greatest poetry lies between them, partaking of both, giving the critic a complex pleasure of discovery and evaluation. It may be, depending upon the nature of the critic's piercing look, that Will poetry and Psyche poetry represent only a small part of the whole, to be enjoined by special pleading, but loved when found. I admit this as a possibility.

Of the two components in our dichotomy, Psyche appears to
be more elusive, to ramify into the more interesting complexities,
to be the harder to grasp since its pleasing quality resides in
its ungraspable part, and by the notion of some kind of grace,
whereby the mind does not wish to probe, nor the intellect to
meddle, but the whole being to accept, when in the grip of
Psyche poetry, thus immediately ceasing to be a critic. But enjoyment may be had either way; there are as many ways of enjoying
poetry as there are ways of living. And I do not say that Psyche
poetry is better than Will poetry. I say that it is more subtle,
more elusive, more delicate, essentially I suspect more over-
whelming by its virtue to take us in against our will, leave us
suspended in delicious realms of ambiguity, unresolved con-
jurations, passive pleasure. It works partially through a religious
attitude.

I have a short poem which appeared in *Reading the Spirit*
in 1937 but which was written I think while I was at Cambridge,
between 1927 and 1929. It was written to the world at large,
to nobody in particular, and was entitled *The Critic*. I wish to
turn this poem upon myself. It goes as follows:

> The Critic with his pained eye
> Cannot my source espy
> For truly and purely to eye it
> He would have as critic to die.
>
> I with joyful vision see,
> I cannot his purpose acquire.
> For if the Critic were truly free
> He would love, and not be a liar.

It may be interesting to quote first a poem which is neither
purely of Will nor of Psyche, but which contains admixtures

of both. I no doubt thought of myself both as poet and critic. I was under the eye of I. A. Richards, and was aware of his early belief that all that modern poetry can do is to make pseudo statements, in fact, tell lies. His psychological point of departure was that in the modern world the scientist alone demonstrates truth; this is the truth of putting one thing to another and calling it, logically enough, two. This is the truth of physical experiment where, given certain facts, certain results must follow. There is rigidity and absolutism. William James enounced this reasonable world in his essay on pragmatism. A thing was good if it worked, which was analogous to the one-to-one conclusions of the experimental scientists. Americans allowed only what worked and now we were becoming great. The assumption was that this was good.

Let us see what my short poem said. It posited in the first line a pained eye for the critic. This is an arbitrary choice of a word, meaningful and setting the mood when quickly followed by the notion that the pained eye of the critic cannot espy or find out the source from which the poet writes. It sets up a dichotomy between poetry and criticism; one is supposed immediately to sympathize with the poet and believe what he says is true. The first stanza ends on the extended notion that the critic would have to die in order to see the source of the poet, or see into it.

The second stanza begins by saying that the poet sees with joyful vision; the assumption is, simply, that the critic does not. In the swiftness of the poem this is supposed to be taken un-challenged. But it is not, of course, necessarily true. The critic is not directly attacked, but the emphasis is placed on the differ-ence of the poet, who cannot "his purpose acquire." Here is a difference, upon contemplation of the poem, that may not at first appear. The critic, in stanza one, might achieve the source

of the poet were he to die as critic. The poem does not specify
the methods for this dying, nor indeed state what kind of dying
it is, psychological or imaginative. But in line two of the second
stanza the poet, because he sees with joyful vision, cannot acquire
the purpose of the critic. This is, in fact, dogmatic assertion
and pleads specially for the poet. It seems to understand instinctively that creation is first and criticism second and that this
is the natural and just order of things. The poem may in fact
be hostile to criticism because of the latter's power, recognized,
but not stated, to be injurious, even deadly to the creation of
poetry. It may therefore arbitrarily assume that the critic has
no joyful vision, which in cold reason nobody would allow, while
the poet has a superior hold on ultimate value. The last two
lines cap off or clinch the central idea of the poem. They say
that if the critic were truly free he would love, and not be a liar.
What gives the poem its life is the terseness and economy of the
expression. Words like "truly" and "purely" are placed, in-
stantaneously, to work efficiently, without the mind having to
stop to ponder them. At the end there is a tacit boon extended
to the critic; in fact, the antilegislation of the first quatrain is
taken back in the "if" proposition which assumes that maybe
the critic can be regenerated. It is not to say that he cannot.
If then in fact he were truly free, he would love, and not be a
liar. The word "love" at the end runs back to the beginning
and ties in the idea of love as intimate to the act of creation,
in poetry here, as well as in fact in nature. Close association
is made between love with its joyful poetic vision and truth.
If the critic were truly free he would not be divorced from the
nature of poetry and he would not have to tell lies about it,
which is his professional business, but by loving he would tell
the truth.

The immediate tone of the poem impresses the obvious dichotomy upon the sensibility; but with reflection and in reading it carefully, it will be seen to be a rather hopeful poem. This ultimately hopeful quality is the Psyche part of the poem, while its thrust and somewhat belligerent immediacy is its Will part. There is the elusive notion that there is something sacrosanct in the source of the poet, which is we may say his Psyche; and, still turning it around, if the critic will exercise Will he may find through love the truth. It seems to me to be neither a true poem of Will nor of Psyche, but to live and persuade with elements of both.

II

Before going into old definitions of Will and Psyche, let me propose two short poems which exemplify some of their characteristics. There is a famous four-line poem, supposed to be sixteenth-century, which many know, an anonymous piece entitled "The Lover in Winter Plaineth for the Spring." It is a poem of the Will.

> O Western wind, when wilt thou blow
> That the small rain down can rain?
> Christ, that my love were in my arms
> And I in my bed again!

This is simple, direct, evocative, a cry from the heart. It is a poem of wish fulfillment as good now as when it was written. It has a positive, strong emotional force. In the death of winter, loveless, the poet longs for spring, which represents love. The ejaculative utterance of the last two lines is powerful. Physical love is celebrated as an absolute good. There is no doubt about

it. Calling upon Christ is a brilliant thrust. The renouncer of
the world is called upon to bring the world most closely home
to the heart. Although exceedingly short, this is a whole poem
written in the fullness of humanity, with ardent belief in life
and in love. It is a direct poem of the Will.

A poem which comes to mind when thinking of Psyche is
Poe's "To Helen," wherein Psyche is named. This is a good
example of Psyche poetry in a pure, or almost pure form. There
is practically no Will in it. If we tend to equate Will poetry
with Romanticism and Psyche poetry with Classicism, this poem
in its form, its balance, and poise, is classical. Poe's emendation
of his lines in the second stanza, to come on " To the glory that
was Greece / And the grandeur that was Rome " is a famous
example of improvement by taking thought. If these words
were written as a prose phrase they would not seem remarkable;
they might pass as journalism. Set as they are, with three major
g's neatly muted by five minor *r*'s, they become memorable.

The poem reads as follows:

To Helen

Helen, thy beauty is to me
　　Like those Nicean barks of yore,
That gently, o'er a perfumed sea,
　　The weary, way-worn wanderer bore
　　To his own native shore.

On desperate seas long wont to roam,
　　Thy hyacinth hair, thy classic face,
Thy Naiad airs have brought me home
　　To the glory that was Greece
And the grandeur that was Rome.

Lo! in yon brilliant window-niche
　　How statue-like I see thee stand,

The agate lamp within thy hand!
Ah! Psyche, from the regions which
Are Holy Land!

Where you feel in our anonymous lover of the sixteenth century his loss of the loved object, and are in no doubt about the strength of his conviction that it would be good to have his love in his arms again, in bed, the reader feels no such strong pull toward its object in this poem. It is a much subtler, finer matter entirely. The poem ends in a sigh, a sort of wistfulness, a recognition that Psyche is so far removed from ordinary affairs that one can only dream about her from afar, not clasp her. She is way off in the improbable distance where her capture would be the remotest possibility. The notion of Psyche as soul is thus intrinsically honored by the poet. This a magical poem, an object of contemplation, having little to do with action.

For all its famed simplicity the poem has a good many ambiguities and subtleties. We are supposed to think of Helen of Troy at once, yet some readers, primitively blessed, may think only of some other Helen. I read this poem for years without knowing what a "Nicean bark" was, and have again by this time forgotten, but this ignorance does not destroy the poem. The main sense is clear. The phrase "weary way-worn wanderer" always struck me as effeminate in the nineteenth-century sense, Swinburnian or late Tennysonian; I have never seen the most fatigued sailor who would fit this description. A plural number is suggested because of the plurality of barks. If they were actually weary and way-worn they would stop wandering, quit, give up, and go home. This is a romantic notion of an improbable kind of sailor, to put you in a mood of dream. We have encountered the notions of gentleness and perfumé already. The barks and the men have actually got home, due to the persuasion of the beauty of Helen, which draws or pulls slowly but inevitably as a tide.

In the second stanza "desperate" is a well-chosen oppositional word and is the only one in the poem that suggests violence of action. The reader has to put up with certain nineteenth-century locutions in the poem, such as "barks of yore," "o'er" as elided, and "wont to roam." These are easily taken in. The first line of the second stanza, "On desperate seas long wont to roam," mounts an ambiguity which is probably not recognized at once by the reader; Helen may be thought to have roamed long on desperate seas as the prize of the Trojan wars, or it may be the poet-reader-adventurer who has done this, the Ulysses spirit. A suspension of meanings involves us in a smooth syllabic flow while we do not have to entertain its underlying mechanisms.

It is obvious that if Poe had transposed "glory" and "grandeur," the poem would not be great. If he had said the "grandeur that was Greece," which would have after all have been possible, "and the glory that was Rome," he would have made a political mistake. The word "glory" has been used for Rome, just as we have our "Glorious Fourth," yet it is elementary that Poe, and probably a lesser poet than Poe would have done the same, perceived "glory" as specially pertaining to Greece, "grandeur" as specially pertaining to Rome. The homing notion of the first stanza is reiterated in a different way. The "hyacinth hair," "classic face," and "Naiad airs" are here the home-bringers, not now just to a native shore, but to the magnitude of spiritual and worldly dynasties.

In the first stanza we do not see Helen, it is not a photograph. It is an intellectual idea. In the third stanza we have a masterful placement, a dichotomy one part of which is a standard conception of a statue in a window-niche, an art object with a certain plastic reality to it, holding aloft an agate lamp, while almost at once this is contraverted by Helen turning into Psyche, " from the regions which / Are Holy Land." There is a great deal of magic cleverly dealt here. First, Helen-Psyche is only " like " a statue, she is " statue-like," so we are in the midst of poetry as a reality shot through with simultaneously-held possibilities. Second, we are invited into a never-never land which takes us unawares, as it were, in the last two lines. They are so finely woven, as is the entire piece, that we accept at once, without the necessity for analysis. The words of the last stanza enforce, in a subtle, gentle way, a mood. The whole poem breathes a mood of gentleness and opens on far contemplations.

For instance, " Lo!," an antique word which we take in stride, is followed by " in yon brilliant window-niche." We do not have to notice the " yon " much, but it is as if a finger were pointing to an actual place, yet poetic vagueness is subsumed, we see no real building; we do not have indication of the architecture if Poe had any in mind; we do not know the material size nor the shape of the window-niche. Poe as magician casually uses the word " brilliant," but this has intellectual implications with regard to the lamp and the meaning of Psyche's light.

" Ah! Psyche " involves us in the ultimate tone of the poem. Psyche, or soul, is from regions which are holy land. The sighing tone of this realization has in it tenderness and longing, yet there is no hint that this sacrosanct reality may be dealt with outright. That is the beauty of the poem. It is Psyche poetry, beyond the will of man. An ultimate reality is addressed. This reality, the soul, is admitted and placed in a true position beyond action. It is a matter almost of religious devotion, at least of religious affinity. Note that in stanza one there was a home coming, in stanza two that there was a further type of home coming, and I had meant to mention the ambiguity of " brought me home," which may refer back to the weary mariners or exist merely as a cant phrase, whereas in the last stanza, as if to progress to the highest spiritual plane of contemplation, there is no action at all, only a serene, ultimate sight to be seen and contemplated, beyond possession, and beyond use. " Holy Land " obviously may refer to the Holy Land and I suppose this sense is to some extent in most readers, intellectually inviting us to impose Jerusalem upon Greece and Rome. One wonders whether Poe intended this. I do not think so. The stress is on " regions." I think as magician-poet he is using valid poetic means, where words taken in usual connotation have overtones of other connotations which may be brought into focus in the mind, or left as a vaguely-felt pleasure. He is having his cake and eating it too to use " holy land " here as the very end of the poem.

The main thing to say about this satisfying poem is that there is a holy land but that we may not get to it. We may contemplate Helen but we may not touch her. If it were a Will poem there could be some anguish because of this fact. Because it is a Psyche poem there is no anguish; the poet is beyond this and the reader is beyond it too. Psyche is the region beyond strife and as Helen it is mythical and fabulous. A light is held on the world. We may contemplate this beauty, which is ultimately impersonal, spiritual, and ineffable.

Sometimes one mumbles certain phrases or lines of a poem in a sort of somnambulistic rite. Sometimes one does this for years. Many poems in English are great because of only a line or a phrase, or a few lines. Almost every school boy has learned " Helen, thy beauty is to me " and if as a man this phrase alone should persist as more memorable than another, it would perhaps be because of his will to violate the poem and possess Helen! If you say "Helen, thy beauty is to me" and stop there you have paid a debt to Poe as poet and as anarchic individualist you have thought to do the impossible, to possess Psyche itself. With that we leave Poe, Helen, and Psyche to the ages. They all age beautifully.

Let me now tell the traditional story of Psyche. It is interesting that the concept of Will has exercised the minds of great thinkers to a great extent and that there is a vast amount of lore on the subject. It is equally interesting, and instructive for our own definitions and distinctions, that encyclopedic notions of Psyche are limited in scope, that there is no vast amount of lore, and that the meanings tend by the nature of the subject to be cast into story, fable, or allegory.

The tale of Cupid and Psyche, in the *Metamorphoses* of Apuleius, is interesting as the only ancient fairy tale which is told as such. In it Psyche, the youngest daughter of a king, arouses the jealousy of Venus, who orders Cupid to inspire her with love for the most despicable of men. "Cupid," continues the *Encyclopaedia Britannica*,

> however, falls in love with her and carries her off to a secluded spot, where he visits her by night, unseen and unrecognized by her. Persuaded by her sisters that her companion is a hideous monster, and forgetful of his warning, she lights a lamp to look upon him while he is asleep; in her ecstasy at his beauty she lets fall a drop of burning oil upon the face of Cupid, who awakes and disappears. Wandering over the earth in search of him, Psyche falls into the hands of Venus, who forces her to undertake the most difficult of tasks. The last and most dangerous of these is to fetch from the world below the box containing the ointment of beauty. She secures the box, but on the way back opens it and is stupified by the

vapour. She is only restored to her senses by Cupid at whose entreaty Jupiter makes her immortal and bestows her in marriage upon her lover.

The Greeks were lucky in living on two planes at once as if there were no contradiction, no dichotomy. They lived in the reality of the earth and in the reality of the heavens. Thus, they were able to invent a pantheon of gods and talk about them as if they were quite like themselves, yet giving them simultaneously the devotions of a different species. Psyche stands for the soul, is a term for the soul, and it is not strange that the Greeks should have told of Psyche in terms of a love story. So the soul and love are intimately allied. And this soul and this love are not so far from immediate concerns as not to have, in the story, all manner of worldly and painful trials, commissions of error, whims of fate; yet the fact remains that the story has a happy ending. The last sentences of the story, as charmingly told by Edith Hamilton (*Mythology*, p. 100) read "So all came to a most happy end. Love and the Soul (for that is what Psyche means) had sought and, after sore trials, found each other; and that union could never be broken." If we say also that poetry is love we have a *raison d'être* for the great amount of Psyche poetry there is in literature. And sometimes, in a plausible moment of illumination, we see things in a clear, fresh way as if for the first time and know that a fairy story with a happy ending is equal to any other interpretation of the world, acceptable as real. Then the obscurity and burden of our minds settles down into our perpetual modern cynical or doubting consciousness.

The fundamental distinction in all the ratiocination of the philosophers about Will is the primary one that it is always stewing in its own juice, is always hoist with its own petard,

is always there in the meshes of the flesh, a bestial or an intellectual thing; whereas the primary qualities of Psyche are harmony, reconciliation, beauty, peace, a timeless at-oneness with
some ultimate value, a fairy story with a happy ending which
is possible only because the idea of Psyche is the most elusive,
the most delicate, the most ephemeral and thus, paradoxically,
the strongest and most complete repository of mortal awareness.
Psyche becomes a myth just as does the Virgin in Christianity.
She is love, as the story was told above, and the fairytale maker
had the penetration to see that his lightness of touch really
embraced and went beyond all the ponderous effects of the
willing animal man. It is possible to take a fairy tale with the
deepest seriousness, it is so wonderful and playful and ultimately
meaningful. But in our time we do not often do so. We think
of ourselves as too realistic.

In our short Will poem about the lover who imprecates
Christ to bring his love to his arms again, we are not concerned
with any part of Psyche. It is physical love that he wants, a total
involvement of flesh and manhood. There is nothing against
this, it is itself a kind of noble charm. But it presupposes that
the lover will be completely joined to him in the kind of love
union he wishes. But in the Psyche story love goes beyond itself
to an airy and ethereal truth, subtle and deep. There is the
suggestion of the danger of looking too deeply into nature in the
lamp-light vigil of Psyche over Cupid. The burning oil is a
sort of fatal flaw which makes the loved object disappear. But
Cupid represents forgiveness at the end of the story and we
note that Psyche is made immortal by a god. This is all beyond
the proper realm of reason. It is unreasonable. It pays implicit
homage to the idea of mystery in human affairs, just as it is true
that in marriage one never knows one's mate and that an elusive

reality is an essence of marriage although it may be practiced for twenty or forty years. With this background, let us return to Will and, while holding judgment in abeyance, throw out some notions of what it is.

There is something about Will which is eternally youthful. The Will, progressing through the flesh with time, a gift of life in its deepest resources of power, has in it all that is wild, free, eager, joyful, the giver and taker of dangers, superior to, while being enmeshed in, all sorts of evils. Will is fresh and lean. Will works beneath the intellect while seeming not to and drives the personality to new action. Will is behind all aggressiveness, all savage deportment. It is there in the subduing of forests, the erecting of cities, the building of armies, acts of war. It gives off death as quickly as it shows forth enlightenment. Brain power is sometimes largely will power. Will is a torment of abuse and the search for perfection. It is a gift of nature. Its symbol could be the impassioned rider spurring the horse. It can dream of universal brotherhood but also of atomic destruction. Cunning, craft, malice, intellect; aspiration, desire, plan, thrust, perseverance, control; faculty, persuasion, peculiarity—these are all willful and are absolutes dominated by the blood-drench, the flow in the veins, the strong life sense, the urgency to dominate, the pleasure of action, the health of a death-violating eye, freedom, and joy.

Freedom and joy! How little freedom and joy there is in the world. They must be made anew, forged in an active principle of blood, in a causative art. This necessity was recognized by Blake, Hopkins, and Lawrence. It is Will that will create the world anew; Will that will make something happen; Will that will make happen the compulsive poems. This also Whitman knew. The Will poet writes with the whole personality in a

full thrust; he is totally engaged in the strength of his realization. A dynamic urgency burns in him; he is alive with vitality,
love and aspiration and malice and scorn. I think of Crane
writing *The Bridge*.

Now we come to a major problem of poetry. Does it conduce
to action? Does it exert a cause from which there must be an
effect? Is it offensive, distasteful, and does it make one wince?
Does it fire one to perhaps even patriotic action? Who would
nowadays think of Longfellow as a revolutionary poet? Yet
was not " Paul Revere's Ride " a revolutionary poem and did not
Americans respond to his " The Ship of State? " Would not
the latter make them ready to die for their country, that is, long
ago? Yeats at one point wanted his poems to spur Irishmen to
militant action.

The Will conduces to the action of the poet in writing the
poem. All poems attempt to persuade in some way. We now
arrive at the problem of communication. And we may as well
go back to our anonymous sixteenth-century short poem of the
poet calling for his love to be in his arms again. I should say
that this sort of successful short poem creates an immediate state
of identification in the reader. The reader has no difficulty in
placing himself in the position of the poet so that he too is
bereft of his lover and with equal passion wishes for the fulfillment cried out for. The poem is universally valid for the
majority of mankind. The reader thus identifies himself with
the material of the poem. It has made something happen in
that it has made the reader feel exactly as the poet felt. We have
to add that the full sway of this poem does not necessarily
bring on the desired result. There is something comical about
a despairing lover. The poem does not say that the desired
result is achieved. It is instead a strong wish-fulfillment; but

I suppose we could hold, without loss of dignity, that if the poet willed strongly enough he would actually find a solution to his difficulties. The poetry has made love happen. Love is the purity of his concern. The problem seems fairly clear in so simple an example. On the other hand, in a Psyche poem like Poe's "To Helen" we have ultimate ambiguity and fluidity, as if the poem lived in a perpetual continuum of unresolved possibilities, whose best communicability is its tempting, fascinating, and endless ability not to give up its secret, not perfectly to communicate, but to float in a magical dew and timeless sight of something seen but not touched, imagined but not possessed, aspired to but not achieved, so that the residue of feeling from this poem is like the feelings about the soul itself. It is a poetic mechanism for preponderating the soul.

III

Let us retrace our steps. The problem of Will and Psyche was announced as a dichotomy, but had hardly so been stipulated than the neatness of this dichotomy was seen to have blurred edges. A search through literature may discover pure poems of Will, as defined, and pure poems of Psyche, as defined, yet the definitions may not be exhaustive and there is a peril that any poem adduced may not be as pure as it seems. The Western Wind poem, about the immediacy of the desired for love, physical love, seems purely of the Will; indeed, it may be quibbling not to think it so. And yet there is the speculation, as one of a problematical number of final connotations, in this case few, that a reservation should be supplied to the intention of the poem; the mind can conceive that it does not go far enough, for nothing is said about the nature or quality or meaning of the love that is cried for in the lover's arms and in bed. We are supposed to blind ourselves to any raveling out of thought. The success of the poem primarily keeps us within bounds; its strong, willful force binds it into a self-contained breathing machine. Except for the critic. The critic may play with these four lines, ranging over them discursive claims. What if the positive thrust of the poem have negative, even disastrous results? There is much love that brings on grief, endless trouble, every form of madness, even suicide, and may give rise to tragic literature. Only a critic would think that there is a lack in the poem because some ultimate result of the predicament is not specified or intimated. Could as great, or as enduring, a poem have been composed, which would also be of the will, if the old Elizabethan had cried out, let us say, in an excess of the kind of manliness that found its exercise and reward in seafaring, new world discovery, or hand-to-hand combat:

> Christ, that my love were never in my arms
> And I in my bed again!

I doubt if the poem would have lasted so long. Yet in the actual poem there is a frustration in the writer which makes it come into being: in my emendation there would also be a frustration, only a different kind of frustration, a modern one. If he were in his bed without his lover, wanting none, but wishing the spring and the rain, he might have recourse to extensive dreams, he might in fact be a performer in the realm of Psyche poetry.

But this gives a comic touch and may perhaps show the limits of criticism. It is not, in a sense, fair to go so far. It is uncalled for. It is not reasonable. Criticism must be based on logic and reason, on scope and judgment. The poem would seem therefore to suggest its own circumference for discussion. If one goes beyond that circle, one is committing bad taste. Bad taste must be excess beyond the facts, that is, sentimentality, and it must be fundamentally wrong-headed. I have produced the above out-of-focus locution to attempt to show that criticism ought to stick to the main course, to look directly at the words and sensible connotations of a poem, not to go off into brainful asides which destroy the cogency and neatness of the suggested poetical system. But I also give it as a warning that the difficulties of criticism are many, and extreme, and that poetry is an unruly horse not easily ridden with elegance.

We then had an example of so-called pure Psyche poetry. Poe's "To Helen" has a restraint, an elegance, a fairness of proportion, which does not invite destruction by easy opposition to make it a willful thing. It stands as an example of enduring, mood-producing, elusive poetry, and the only comment I have finally to make on it in the context of our subject, is that, however tender and wistful and suggestive its ultimate feeling may be, Poe yet had the will to write it. So the problem is still there. If he had only day-dreamed the poem, not composed it by strict, calculating, and masterful art, we should be the losers by his lack of will.

It is possible to think simply and clearly. Perhaps the great thinkers have done so. It is also possible, and just as human, to think unclearly and in a profusion of confusions, jumping this way and that, going off on tangents, trying to grasp meanings out of the air, so to speak, and great thinkers have done this. Life is complex; a famous apology for complexity in modern poetry is that it is so because modern life is complex. There is a sort of tenacity in the mind to resist conclusion. To conclude is to arrive beyond Will at stasis and finality. It is the Romantic point that to strive is better than to arrive; the struggle toward definition is more rewarding than whatever may be gained from final conclusion. Hell is more interesting than heaven; evil more provocative than good. But I suppose it depends upon the age, the age's characteristics. The eighteenth century provided a static society, a well-ordered and neat outlook on life; thus came didacticism in Pope and Dryden. The nineteenth century brought on the hidden beast in the machine, so we had the rumblings and exalted strikes-through of Romantic, assertive individualism. The twentieth century brought to flower in its first half a monstrous bloom of societal chaos, so we have a great poem like "The Waste Land" in a nonassertive revolution of intentions which penetrated into the surrounding chaos itself and brought forth chaotic resolutions.

What is a Psyche state in poetry? I would wish to continue without definition, dwelling in an ambience of vagueness, willfully shirking the duty of defining heaven. I would like to have my Psychic cake and eat it too, and not tell what it is made of! I would like to advance the cause of subtlety, mystery, and the ineffable. However, one cannot talk to no purpose, thinking runs to conclusion, and it is a pleasure to don the mantle of a sometime critic, from which I state, simply, that a Psyche state in poetry pertains to, exemplifies, or takes off from peace, quiet, calm, security, harmony, proportion, concord, tranquillity, freedom as from something (war, for instance), serenity, stillness and silence. Now to give Will its same and simple due. Will is wish, desire, inclination, pleasure, appetite, passion, purpose, determination, choice, intention, entreaty, command, decree, power, arbitrary disposal, self-control as in a man of strong will, zeal, volition.

I wish to be clearly understood in this paper that my dichotomy is arbitrary, existing as a framework for the discussion of works of poetry fitted more or less arbitrarily into my scheme because of my love of the poems chosen. I make no claim as a philosopher to any new original concept about Will and am in fact in awe of all the heavy ratiocination about this term in the history of philosophy. Likewise of Psyche I do not write a new story of Psyche to equal the Greek. On both of these terms I have levied my own definitions, but I like to resist conclusions because there can be no real conclusion to literary criticism. It is a living, breathing, continuing thing.

Then also I want to make it clear, at the risk of repeating, that literary criticism is not a science, cannot be accurate in the way that a physical experiment may be accurate, and has its pleasures in a humane attitude to what is at hand. Ambiguity is one of the charms of modern poetical criticism. I entered these delighting reaches early. While I was at Cambridge, my classmate William Empson was writing, as a man in his early twenties, that seminal book *Seven Types of Ambiguity*. I want to conclude, very shortly, with an anecdote of what happened to a Roman poet who wrote an ambiguous line under Caius Caligula.

But we have to deal with literary criticism. Therefore it seems sensible in this paper to give you some added notions about it. Of the types of poetical criticism the evaluative is best. It represents a lofty attitude. When practiced by a judicious, not a prejudiced mind, the results may be salutary. When practiced by prejudiced minds, the criticism is thrown down into the arena of politics. Politics is the low view, moiled in human error. Political criticism has little or low value. It does not aim at the truth, nor at justice, but at chance, distraction, and temporality. This is not to say that political criticism should be outlawed. We must suffer it along with the greatest. It is part of the stability of democracy to entertain it. But the intention is impure.

The intention of evaluative criticism, in a judicious mind, is high. It strives to seek the truth about a work of art and to communicate this truth to the reader. All manner of subtleties of perceptions are available to this type of criticism. It does not rule out a-priori scaffolding, which accounts in part for Dr. Johnson; nor does it rule out elusive intellectual concretions, which specifies, sometimes, Coleridge. It does not say that the New Criticism necessarily has the last word in any ramifying arguments, neither does it allow that the neo-Aristoteleans have the last word. Evaluative criticism in an honest and perceptive mind seeks to establish life-giving relationships within the art and between art and society. It neither wishes to overpraise nor to underrate. It may propose unwitting prejudices in the very structure of mind, in that mind is always idiosyncratic; the reader allows for this and in reading Empson, for instance, much of the fun is in acceptance of his peculiarities of temperament which give on to the liveliness of his sometimes far-fetched presentations. Yet few would say that, totally speaking, he was not devoted to finding out the truth about a literary work. It takes some wit to appreciate wit.

I have no objection to categorical criticism, and assume we have yet to see a totally categorical criticism mastering the entire aesthetic intentions of the West; the field is so vast and wide none has yet had the arbitrary ability to contain it. Dante in his *Commedia* wrote the best criticism of the medieval time, but in a sense it seems too easy: his world was unified. Goethe had a harder task and did less well. Eliot in our time leaned upon modern Christianity and seemed to take in not the whole, but parts. His view has the feel of the limited. It beguiled us for

decades but, as Mr. Blackmur perceptively remarked, we tend
to read "Four Quartets" instead of the Bible. We get the
Bible through modern religious poetry. There is something very
wrong about this. Dante's work was so happily integrated with
the total religious integration of his times that one has no feeling
of this sort of substitution when reading the *Commedia*. Perhaps
this was a lucky and happy fall of historical events, that is all.

It may be that the *aperçu*, the unschematized, personal intuition is as good a type as any, maybe better than most, in our
present state of taste. Students tend to rebel, for instance, at
Yeats' hard-won schematization in "A Vision" which, although
fascinating, fails to satisfy due to arbitrariness and straining.
Few really love it. Many can admire its conic elaborations but
it somehow does not take in all of life. They give it admiration,
along with understanding, but they do not give it love, which it
does not invite. It may be that the relatively few, somewhat
undisciplined, but thoroughly human asides, chance perceptions,
and penetrating remarks by Frost represent the best criticism
about poetry, a criticism not of a school, also not eccentric, but
wise flashes of truth thrown off easily, if sparingly, down the
decades. Too much criticism is a noose around the neck of
creation. Each reader should be his own critic, should be strong
to hold in abeyance final judgment on any criticism, lest he lose
his soul. I propose abeyance criticism. It points up enjoyment,
tones down tomb-cold finalities. Let us keep the doors of
perception open.

Now we know the bold outlines of our dichotomy and we see
that much pleasure of poetry resides in ambiguity, that Will and
Psyche conjoin to destroy any simple black-and-white approach
to them, and we will find, perhaps, a great difficulty in ever
getting beyond the idea that ambiguity is a prime source of

pleasure in the art of poetry; that vagueness and irresolution are values leading to possibilities of prolonged enjoyment; and that nothing ultimate about poetry can be scientifically clear.

Yet in ancient Rome a poet lost his life because of ambiguity. It is in a somewhat facetious mood that I conclude by presenting the Emperor Caius Caligula as critic, absolute and mad. This wild man lived twenty-nine years (A.D. 12-41) but fortunately ruled only three years, ten months and eight days, according to Suetonius. Our historian says, " He burned a writer of Atellan farces alive in the middle of the arena of the amphitheater, because of a humorous line of double meaning. When a Roman knight on being thrown to the wild beasts loudly protested his innocence, he took him out, cut off his tongue, and put him back again."

May our American critics be never as fierce as Caligula, and may I not have the will to cut off anybody's tongue in my criticism.

Richard Wilbur

Round About

A Poem of

Housman's

IN THE SPRING OF 1944 MY division was withdrawn from action and assigned to a rest area not far from Naples. Once we had pitched our tents, painted our tent-pegs white, cleaned and polished our equipment, and generally recovered the garrison virtues, we were allowed to make occasional excursions, in groups of one truckload, to nearby points of interest. I remember best our trip to Pompeii. One reason why I remember it so clearly is that, on the day of our visit, Vesuvius began its worst eruption in many decades. Our six-by-six truck approached Pompeii through a fine, steady fall of whitish flakes, and set us down in a square already carpeted with ash. Some of our party, not caring for archeology, headed directly for the bars and other comforts of the modern city; but the rest of us thought it more seemly to begin, at least, with a look at the ruins. We found a displaced Greek woman who offered to be our guide, and she took us through the greater part of the excavations, pointing out the wall paintings, deciphering inscriptions, explaining the water system—until at last, just as we reached the Greek Forum, there was a sudden darkening of the air, a thickening in the fall of ashes, and she took fright and left us.

We found our way back to the modern city and established ourselves in a bar, sitting near the window so that we could watch for the return of our truck. The street was now full of natives evacuating the place, wading through the ashes under the usual clumsy burdens of refugees. Sitting there with a brandy bottle and watching such a scene, we felt something like the final tableau of *Idiot's Delight*. There were jokes about how we had better look smart and sit straight, since we might have to hold our poses for centuries. And one bookish soldier said that he had never felt so close to Pliny the Elder.

Before we had exhausted that vein of nervous humor, the truck arrived, and our scattered party emerged or was extricated from all the bars and dives of the vicinity. Climbing over the tailgate, most of us had some trophy or memento to show or show around: one had a bottle of Marsala, another a bottle of grappa; one had an album of colored views of the ruins; another drew from that breast-pocket which is supposed to carry a bullet-proof New Testament a packet of French postcards. And then there were cameos from Naples, and salamis, and pure silk placemats marked *Ricordo d'Italia*. When everything had been shown and assessed, one slightly drunken soldier leaned forward on his bench and said, "All right, boys, now you look at *this*." He held out his fist, opened it, and there on his palm stood a small, good replica of the famous sculpture of the wolf, nursing Romulus and Remus.

"How *about* that?" he said. "Man, ain't that the dirtiest got-damn statue you ever saw?"

I don't tell that in ridicule of the soldier who said it. He

had been a good farmer in East Texas, and he was a good soldier
in Italy; his talk had more verve, rhythm, and invention in it—
more poetry in it—than one usually hears in the talk of cultured
people; and I would not call him inferior, as a man, to the soldier
who happened to know that Pliny the Elder was done in by
Vesuvius. I tell the story because, in this hopeful democracy of
ours, in which the most unpromising are coerced into a system
of free public education, we must often remind ourselves that
the art public is not coextensive with the population, or even
with the voting population. Any poet would feel justified in
referring to Romulus and Remus and the wolf—one could hardly
find a classical allusion more safely commonplace; and yet there
really are millions of Americans who would not understand the
reference, and who really might, if they saw the Wolf of the
Capitol, mistake it for a dirty statue. We must stubbornly
remember this whenever polemicists began to strike the Whitman note, and to ask for a poetry at once serious and universally
understandable.

A young Japanese woman told me recently of a parlor game
which she and her friends had often played: fragmentary quotations from haiku are written on slips of paper; the slips of paper
are put into a box; and then each player draws in his turn, reads
out the fragment, and attempts to say the complete seventeen-
syllable poem from memory. When cultured young Japanese
play such a game as that, they are drawing on a detailed acquaintance with a vast haiku literature reaching back more than seven
hundred years. And this acquaintance has to do with far more
than subject matter. Haiku literature is, for instance, full of
plum blossoms; and in order to see the uniqueness of a fragment
having to do with plum blossoms one would have to possess
not only a sense of the total history of that motif in Japanese

verse, but also an intimate familiarity with the norms of diction, the strategies of suggestion and the modes of feeling which belong to the haiku convention and to its great practitioners. It goes without saying that any modern Japanese poet who writes a haiku can expect his best readers to grasp his every echo, variation, or nuance.

It is both good and bad that for American poets and their clientele there exists no such distinct, subtle, and narrow tradition. Our cultural and literary traditions are longer and far more inclusive than the Japanese, but they shape our lives far less decidedly and are subject to perpetual revision. A professor planning the reading list for a freshman Humanities course scratches his head and wonders whether St. Augustine's conception of history is in any way relevant to our own; one critic decides that our present sense of the past can do without Milton and Shelley, while another discovers that the main line of poetic tradition does, after all, lead through Alexander Pope. Similarly, our poets have shifting and rival conceptions of what the "tradition" is, and this leads in practice to a constant renewal, modification, and blending of conventions. What's good about this situation is that our poetry is not conventionally inhibited from coping with modern life as it comes; the modern poem is an adaptable machine that can run on any fuel whatever. The obvious disadvantage is that our unstable sense of literary tradition, and our dissolving multiplicity of conventions, makes it hard for the educated person not a devotee of poetry to develop *tact.*

A tactful person is one who understands not merely what is said, but also what is meant. In a spring issue of the *New Republic*, a correspondent described the melancholy experience of exposing a class of engineers to a well-known four-line poem by Ogden Nash—the one that goes

> Candy
> Is dandy,
> But liquor
> Is quicker.

As I recall, the article said that only one student in the lot recognized that poem as humor. The others either had no response or took it to be a straight-faced admonitory poem about obesity, blood sugar, or some such thing. Now, it is true that contemporary poets, encouraged by the critical rediscovery of the seriousness of wit, have done much to confound the distinction between light verse and serious poetry. Think how light Robert Frost can be, even in a quite serious poem; and think how often Phyllis McGinley trespasses on the serious. Still, it is a terrible failure of tact to read Mr. Nash's poem with a long face. The little jingly lines, the essentially comic rhymes, and the slangy diction combine to require that we place it within the convention of light verse. From a certainty as to the convention we derive a certainty as to tone, and when we know the tone we know what the subject must be: Mr. Nash is writing about strategies of seduction, a topic on which Americans incline to be coy, and his leaving the subject unstated is equivalent to a wink and a dig in the ribs.

Even in poems where the subject is fully stated, there is a world of difference between what is said and what is meant, and this I should like to prove by a brief absurd example. There is a charming popular song called "Paper Moon," the first eight bars of which go as follows:

> Say, it's only a paper moon
> Sailing over a cardboard sea
> But it wouldn't be make believe
> If you believed in me

I want now to juxtapose those lines with a passage from Matthew Arnold's " Dover Beach." That poem begins, as you'll remember,

> The sea is calm tonight,
> The tide is full, the moon lies fair
> Upon the straits . . .

and then it proceeds toward this climactic passage:

> Ah, love, let us be true
> To one another! for the world, which seems
> To lie before us like a land of dreams,
> So various, so beautiful, so new,
> Hath really neither joy, nor love, nor light,
> Nor certitude, nor peace, nor help for pain.

It would be possible, I submit, to compose a one-sentence paraphrase which would do for both " Paper Moon " and " Dover Beach." It might go something like this: " The lover begs his beloved to cleave to him, and thus alleviate through human love his painful sense of the meaninglessness of the modern world, here symbolized by the false beauty of the moon." What I have just done is scandalous, of course; but I hope you will agree that it proves something. It proves that if we consider statement only, and work upon it with the disfiguring tool of paraphrase, a frisky pop-song and a tragic poem can be made to seem identical. From this one can see how much of the meaning of any poem resides in its sound, its pacing, its diction, its literary references, its convention—in all those things which we must apprehend by tact.

One of my favorite poems of A. E. Housman is called " Epitaph on an Army of Mercenaries," and because it is a soluble problem in tact I want to discuss it here. Let me say it to you a first time in a fairly flat voice, so as to stress by *lack* of stress

the necessity, at certain points, of making crucial decisions as
to tone:

> These, in the day when heaven was falling,
> The hour when earth's foundations fled,
> Followed their mercenary calling,
> And took their wages and are dead.
>
> Their shoulders held the sky suspended;
> They stood, and earth's foundations stay;
> What God abandoned, these defended,
> And saved the sum of things for pay.

Perhaps the main decision to be made is, how to say those
last two words, "for pay." Should they be spoken in a weary
drawl? Should they be spoken matter-of-factly? Or should they
be spat out defiantly, as if one were saying "Of *course* they did
it for pay; what did you expect?" Two or three years ago, I
happened to mention Housman's poem to a distinguished author
who is usually right about things, and he spoke very ill of it.
He found distasteful what he called its easy and sweeping
cynicism, and he thought it no better, except in technique, than
the more juvenile pessimistic verses of Stephen Crane. For him,
the gist of the poem was this: "What a stinking world this is,
in which what we call civilization must be preserved by the
blood of miserable hirelings." And for him, that last line was
to be said in a tone of wholesale scorn:

> And saved the *sum of things* for *pay*.

I couldn't accept that way of taking the poem, even though
at the time I was unprepared to argue against it; and so I per-
sisted in saying Housman's lines to myself, in my own way,
while walking or driving or waiting for trains. Then one day I
came upon an excellent essay by Cleanth Brooks, which sup-

ported my notion of the poem and expressed its sense and tone far better than I could have done. Mr. Brooks likened Housman's Shropshire lads, so many of whom are soldiers, to those Hemingway heroes who do the brave thing not out of a high idealism but out of stoic courage and a commitment to some personal or professional code. Seen in this manner, Housman's mercenaries—his professional soldiers, that is—are not cynically conceived; rather their poet is praising them for doing what they had engaged to do, for doing what had to be done, and for doing it without a lot of lofty talk. If we understand the poem so, it is not hard to see what tones and emphases are called for:

> *These*, in the day when heaven was falling
> The hour when earth's foundations fled,
> Followed their mercenary calling,
> And took their wages and are dead.
>
> *Their* shoulders held the sky suspended;
> *They stood*, and earth's foundations stay;
> What God abandoned, *these defended*,
> And saved the sum of things for pay.

That is how I would read it, and I suspect that Mr. Brooks would concur. But now suppose that the distinguished author who thought the poem wholly cynical should not be satisfied. Suppose he should say, "Mr. Brooks' interpretation is very enhancing, and makes the poem far less cheaply sardonic; but unfortunately Mr. Brooks is being more creative than critical, and the poem is really just what I said it was."

There are a number of arguments I might venture in reply, and one would be this: Housman was a great classical scholar, and would have been particularly well acquainted with the convention of the military epitaph. His title refers us, in fact, to such poems as Simonides wrote in honor of the Spartans who fell at Thermopylae, or the Athenians who fought at the Isthmus. Those poems are celebratory in character, and so is Housman's. The sound and movement of Housman's poem accord, moreover, with the mood of plain solemnity which the convention demands. The tetrameter, which inclines by its nature to skip a bit, and which we have already encountered in "Oh, it's only a paper moon," is slowed down here to the pace of a dead-march. The rhetorical balancing of line against line, and half-line against half-line, the frequency of grammatical stops, and the even placement of strong beats, make a deliberate movement inescapable; and this deliberate movement releases the full and powerful sonority which Housman intends. It is not the music of sardony.

The distinguished author might come back at me here, saying something like this: "No doubt you've named the right convention, but what you forget is that there are *mock*-versions of every convention, including this one. While Housman's mock-use of the military epitaph is not broadly comic but wryly subtle, it does employ the basic trick of high burlesque. Just as Pope, in his mock-epic *The Rape of the Lock*, adopts the tone and matter of Milton or Homer only to deflate them, so Housman sets his solemn, sonorous poem to leaking with the word 'mercenary,' and in the last line lets the air out completely. The poem is thus a gesture of total repudiation, a specimen of indiscriminate romantic irony, and it's what we might expect from the poet who counsels us to 'endure an hour and see injustice done,' who refers to God as 'whatever brute and blackguard made the world,' and who disposes of this life by crying, 'Oh, why did I awake? When shall I sleep again?'"

From now on I am going to play to win, and I shall not allow

the distinguished author any further rebuttals. The answer to
what he said just now is this: while Housman may maintain
that "heaven and earth ail from the prime foundation," he
consistently honors those who face up manfully to a bad world;
and especially he honors the common soldier who, without
having any fancy reasons for doing so, draws his mercenary
"thirteen pence a day" and fights and dies. We find this soldier
in such poems as "Lancer," or "Grenadier," and Housman
always says to him,

> dead or living, drunk or dry,
> Soldier, I wish you well.

The mercenaries of the poem I've been discussing are enlisted
from all these other soldier-poems, and though their deaths
exemplify the world's evil, Housman stresses not that but the
shining of their courage in the general darkness.

The poem is not a mock-version of the military epitaph; however, the distinguished author was right in feeling that Housman's poem is not so free of irony as, for instance, William
Collins' eighteenth-century ode, "How sleep the brave . . ."
These eight short lines do, in fact, carry a huge freight of irony,
most of it implicit in a system of subtle echoes and allusions;
but none of the irony is at the expense of the mercenaries, and
all of it defends them against slight and detraction.

If one lets the eye travel over Housman's lines, looking for
echo or allusion, it is probably line 4 which first arrests the
attention:

> And took their wages and are dead.

This puts one in mind of St. Paul's Epistle to the Romans,
Chapter VI, where the Apostle declares that "the wages of sin
is death." The implication of this echo is that paid professional

soldiers are sinful and unrighteous persons, damned souls who
have forfeited the gift of eternal life. That is certainly not
Housman's view, even if one makes allowance for ironic exaggera-
tion; and so we are forced to try and imagine a sort of person
whose view it might be. The sort of person we're after is, of
course, self-righteous, idealistic, and convinced of his moral
superiority to those common fellows who fight, not for high and
noble reasons, but because fighting is their job. Doubtless you've
heard regulars of the American army subjected to just that kind
of spiritual snobbery, and one readily finds analogies in other
departments of life: think of the way professional politicians are
contemned by our higher-minded citizens, while shiny-faced
amateurs are prized for their wholesome incapacity. Spiritual
snobs are unattractive persons under any circumstances, but they
appear to especial disadvantage in Housman's poem. After all,
they and their civilization were saved by the mercenaries—or
professionals—who did their fighting for them, and that fact
makes their scorn seem both ungrateful and hypocritical.

Housman's echo of St. Paul, then, leads us to imagine a class
of people who look down on Tommy Atkins, and it also prompts
us to defend Tommy Atkins against their unjust disdain. Let
me turn now to some other echoes, to a number of Miltonic
reverberations which are scattered throughout the poem. They
all derive from some ten lines of the Sixth Book of *Paradise
Lost*. That is the book about the war in heaven, wherein the
good angels and the rebel angels fight two great and inconclusive
engagements, after which the Messiah enters and single-handedly
drives the rebels over the wall of heaven. It is probably not
irrelevant to mention that the ruling idea of Book VI, the idea
which all the action illustrates, is that might derives from right,
and that righteousness therefore must prevail. Here is a passage

which comes at the end of the second battle, when the good and
bad angels are throwing mountains at each other:

> . . . horrid confusion heapt
> Upon confusion rose: and now all Heav'n
> Had gone to wrack, with ruin overspread,
> Had not th' Almighty Father where he sits
> Shrin'd in his Sanctuary of Heav'n secure,
> Consulting on the sum of things, foreseen
> This tumult, and permitted all, advis'd (668 ff.).

The sum of things means here the entire universe, including
heaven and hell, and God is about to save the sum of things
by sending his son against the rebel angels. Otherwise heaven
might fall, and earth's foundations might flee. When the
Messiah drives Satan and his forces over heaven's edge, and they
begin their nine-day fall into hell, Milton gives us another
passage which Housman has echoed:

> Hell heard the unsufferable noise, Hell saw
> Heav'n ruining from Heav'n, and would have fled
> Affrighted; but strict Fate had cast too deep
> Her dark foundations, and too fast had bound (867 ff.).

It's quite plain that Housman is reminding his reader of
Milton, and in particular of these two passages from Book VI, in
which we find "the sum of things," fleeing foundations, and
heaven in peril of falling. The ticklish question now is, how
much of Milton should we put into Housman's poem; how
detailed a comparison should we draw between the war in
Milton's heaven and the battle in which Housman's mercenaries
died? Should we, for instance, compare Housman's sacrificial
mercenaries, whose deaths have preserved the sum of things,
to the Son of God who won the war in heaven and later died

on earth to save mankind? Housman is quite capable of implying such a comparison. In his poem "The Carpenter's Son," Christ is a Shropshire lad who dies on the gallows because he would not "leave ill alone." And in the poem " 1887," Housman says this of the soldiers who have helped God save the Queen by dying in battle:

> To skies that knit their heartstrings right,
>   To fields that bred them brave,
> The saviours come not home to-night:
>   Themselves they could not save.

As Mr. Brooks points out in his essay, those last lines "echo the passage in the Gospels in which Christ, hanging on the cross, is taunted with the words: 'Others he saved; himself he cannot save.'" It appears, then, that in his "Epitaph on an Army of Mercenaries" Housman may be bestowing on his soldiers the ultimate commendation; he may be saying that their sacrifice, in its courage and in the scope of its consequences, was Christlike. For the rest, I should say that Housman's Miltonic allusions have a clear derogatory purpose, and that their function is once again to mock those who feel superior to the soldiers whom the poet wishes to praise. Housman mocks those who feel that they are on the side of the angels, that their enemies are devils, that God is their property and will defend the right, that heaven and earth depend upon their ascendancy and the prevalence of their lofty mores, yet who count in fact not on God or on themselves but on the courage of mercenaries whom they despise.

These smug people, whom the poem nowhere mentions but everywhere rebukes, are covertly attacked again in line five through an allusion to the eleventh labor of Heracles. In that enterprise, Heracles was out to secure the golden apples of the Hesperides, and he applied for the help of Atlas, the giant who supports the heavens on his shoulders. Atlas agreed to go and get the apples, if Heracles would temporarily take over his burden. When Atlas returned, he noticed that Heracles was supporting the heavens very capably, and it occurred to him that Heracles might well continue in the assignment. Had Heracles not then thought of a good stratagem, and tricked Atlas into reassuming the weight of the skies, he would have been the victim of the greatest buck-passing trick on record. What Housman is saying by way of this allusion is that the battle of his poem was won not on the playing fields of Eton but in the pastures of Shropshire, and that the Etonians, and the other pillars of the established order, transferred their burden in this case to the lowly professional army. Once we recognize Housman's reference, we can see again the extent of his esteem for the so-called mercenaries: he compares them to the great Heracles. And once we perceive that line five has to do with buck-passing, with the transference of a burden, we know where to place the emphasis. It should fall on the first word:

> *Their* shoulders held the sky suspended.

It was *they*, the mercenaries, and not the presumptive upholders of the right, who saved the day.

It seems to me that quite enough allusions have now been found; there may be others, but if so we don't need them for purposes of understanding. Nor, I think, do we need to consider the possible fiscal overtones of the words "saved" and "sum." It's true that in conjunction with the words "wages" and "pay," the phrase "saved the sum" has a slight clink of money in it, and one could probably think up an appropriate meaning for such a play on words. But readers and critics must be careful not to be cleverer than necessary; and there is no greater obtuseness than to treat all poets as Metaphysicals, and to insist on discovering puns which are not likely to be there.

What I've been trying to illustrate, no doubt too exhaustively, is how a reader might employ tact in arriving at a sure sense of an eight-line poem. Probably I've gone wrong here or there: I'm afraid, for one thing, that I've made the poem seem more English and less universal than it is. But I hope at any rate to have considered some of the things which need considering: the convention of the poem; the use of the convention; the sound, pace, and tone of the poem; its consistency with the author's attitudes and techniques in other poems; and the implicit argument of its allusions or echoes. Let me read it a last time:

> These, in the day when heaven was falling,
> The hour when earth's foundations fled,
> Followed their mercenary calling,
> And took their wages and are dead.
>
> Their shoulders held the sky suspended;
> They stood, and earth's foundations stay;
> What God abandoned, these defended,
> And saved the sum of things for pay.

Karl Shapiro has lately published in *Poetry* magazine a prose outburst with which I greatly sympathize and yet thoroughly disagree. I won't aim to answer it as a whole, because as he himself says it is too inconsistent to constitute a clear target. You can, within limits, argue with a wild man; wild men are simple; but there's no arguing with a subtle and reasonable man who is bent on being wild. Let me, however, quote one passage from Mr. Shapiro which bears on what I've been saying. He objects to the fact that in our country the only poetry that is recognized is the poetry that repeats the past, that is referential. It relates back to books, to other poetry, to names in the encyclopaedia. It is the poetry of the history-inhibited mind only, and as such it is meaningless to people who lack the training to read it. The Little Magazine, the avant-gardist, the culture academician base the esthetic experience on education. Whereas poetry needs not education or culture but the open perceptions of the healthy human organism.

Mr. Shapiro and I agree that a poem which refers to Romulus and Remus and the wolf will be meaningless, in part at least, to those who lack the training to read it. I disagree, however, with Mr. Shapiro's determination to hound that wolf out of poetry, to abolish the literary and historical past, to confine us to the modern city and declare the ruins off-limits. It would not be worth it to make poetry more generally usable at the cost of abridging the poet's consciousness.

I will say, parenthetically, that I wish the category of expertly-made popular poetry had not all but disappeared in this century. In the last century, the best poets did not hesitate to write on occasion simple songs, hymns, or story-poems which were instantly possessed and valued by a larger public. The author of "In Memoriam" also wrote the ballad of "The Revenge." Though societies were formed to unravel the knottier verses of Robert Browning, there are no knots in "The Pied Piper of Hamelin." I think too of James Russell Lowell's "Once to Every Man and Nation," and of Longfellow's "Paul Revere." These are all fine poems, and all of them are perfectly transparent. Perhaps it is their very transparency which has led critics and teachers to fall silent about them, there being no call for learned mediation; and perhaps that silence has helped many of our poets to forget that there is such a thing as a good popular poem.

But now let me take Housman's poem as a miniature specimen of what Mr. Shapiro calls "high art," and defend it against Mr. Shapiro. It is probably not Housman whom Mr. Shapiro is attacking, and yet the strictures might all apply to him. Mr. Shapiro talks as if a poem could be either referential or humanly vital, but not both. Surely you will agree that Housman's poem is both: it is a passionate celebration of courage, prompted one suspects by an immediate occasion; at the same time, and without any dampening of its urgency, it recalls a convention as old as the Greeks, and defends its heroes against detraction through liberal allusions to literature and myth. Mr. Shapiro says that to be referential is to "repeat the past"; Housman most certainly does not do that. What he does is to confront the present with a mind and heart which contain the past. His poem does not knuckle under to a Greek convention, it makes use of that convention and much modifies it. His allusions do not "repeat" Milton and St. Paul, they bring them to bear upon a contemporary event, and in turn they bring that event to bear upon Milton and St. Paul. Milton's good angels are not, in Housman's poem, what they were in *Paradise Lost*; they are transformed by a fresh conjunction; and Housman implicitly quarrels both with the moral exclusiveness of St. Paul and with Milton's idea that righteousness must prevail.

I would uphold Housman's poem as a splendid demonstration of the art of referring. The poem requires a literate reader, but given such a reader it is eminently effective. I selected the poem for discussion precisely because, unlike most of Housman, it is capable of misinterpretation; nevertheless, as I've pointed out, a reader *can* arrive at a just sense of its tone and drift without consciously identifying any of its references. It *all but* delivers its whole meaning right away. One reason why Housman's allusions can be slow in transpiring, as they were for me, is that the words which point toward Milton or St. Paul—such words as "wages" or "earth's foundations"—are perfectly at home in the language of the poem as a whole; and this seems to me a great virtue. In a bad poem, there are often certain words which step out of line, wave their arms, and cry "Follow me! I have overtones!" It takes a master to make references, or what Robert Frost calls "displacements," without in any way falsifying the poem's voice, its way of talking. Now, as for the allusions proper, they are to the Bible, *Paradise Lost*, and Greek mythology, all of which are central to *any* version of our tradition, and in some degree familiar to every educated reader. So familiar are these sources that I'm sure Housman's allusions must unconsciously affect anyone's understanding of the poem, even upon a casual first reading. And I would say that our familiarity with the things to which Housman is referring justifies the subtlety and brevity of his echoes. The poem assumes that the words "wages" and "dead" will suffice to suggest St. Paul, and I think that a fair assumption.

Housman's allusions, once one is aware of them, are not decorative but very hard working. Their chief function is to supplement Housman's explicit praise of the mercenaries with implicit dispraise of their detractors, and so make us certain of the poem's whole attitude toward its subject. To achieve such certainty, however, one need not catch every hint, every echo; any *one* of Housman's references, rightly interpreted, will permit the reader to take confident possession of the poem. I like that. A poem should not be like a double-crostic; it should not be the sort of puzzle in which you get nothing until you get it all. Art doesn't or shouldn't work that way; we are not cheated of a symphony if we fail to react to some passage on the flute, and a good poem should yield itself more than once, offering the reader an early and sure purchase, and deepening repeatedly as he comes to know it better.

This is what happens time and again as one reads and re-reads Housman. In his poem, "On the Idle Hill of Summer," an indolent young man hears the stirring and fatal music of a marching column, and decides to enlist. The final quatrain goes like this:

> Far the calling bugles hollo,
> High the screaming fife replies,
> Gay the files of scarlet follow;
> Woman bore me, I will rise.

"Woman bore me, I will rise." He will rise and enlist because "woman bore him"—that is, because he is a man and can't resist the summons of the bugle. The last line is forceful and plain, and clinches the poem beautifully. We need no more. Yet there is more, and perhaps on the second reading, or the fifth, or the twentieth, we may hear in that last line a reverberation of the prayer which is said at the graveside in the Anglican burial service, and which begins: "Man, that is born of a woman, hath but a short time to live, and is full of misery . . ."

If we do catch that echo, the line gains both in power and in point; but if we don't catch it, we are still possessed of a complete and trustworthy version of Housman's poem. And to speak again of Milton, I think that most of the reverberations in *Paradise Lost* work in the same way. Satan, wakening in the fiery gulf of Hell, says to Beelzebub, who is sprawled at his side:

> If thou beest he; But O how fall'n! how chang'd
> From him, who in the happy Realms of Light
> Cloth'd with transcendent brightness didst outshine
> Myriads though bright . . .

There is a suggestion of Isaiah there which perhaps I might notice unassisted; but I lack the ready knowledge of Virgil which Milton reasonably expected of his reader, and so I am grateful for the scholar's footnote which directs me to Book II of the *Aeneid*. There the shade of Hector appears to Aeneas in a dream, mangled, blackened with dirt, and *quantum mutatus ab illo Hectore*—"how changed" from that Hector who once returned from battle clothed in the bright armor of Achilles! The Virgilian echo is enhancing; it helps to tune the voice of Satan, and the likening of Beelzebub to Hector poignantly stresses the rebel angels' fall from brightness and from heroic strength and virtue. But if there were no footnote to help me, if I never sensed the shade of Hector behind Milton's lines, I should not on that account be balked or misled. I should already have gathered from the surface of the lines one sure and adequate sense of their tone and meaning.

Let me now read you a more dubious example of the art of referring. The poem is by Yeats; it was written in 1909 or 1910, after the poet's reconciliation with Maud Gonne; and its title is "King and No King."

> "Would it were anything but merely voice!"
> The No King cried who after that was King,
> Because he had not heard of anything
> That balanced with a word is more than noise;
> Yet Old Romance being kind, let him prevail
> Somewhere or somehow that I have forgot,
> Though he'd but cannon—Whereas we that had thought

To have lit upon as clean and sweet a tale
Have been defeated by that pledge you gave
In momentary anger long ago;
And I that have not your faith, how shall I know
That in the blinding light beyond the grave
We'll find so good a thing as that we have lost?
The hourly kindness, the day's common speech,
The habitual content of each with each
When neither soul nor body has been crossed.

A great many intelligent readers, including some professional poets of my acquaintance, have found this poem very troublesome. In order to fathom its sixteen lines, one must follow the suggestion of Yeats' title and read *A King and No King*, which is a five-act play by Beaumont and Fletcher first performed in 1611. The play tells how King Arbaces of Iberia conceives an incestuous passion for his sister Panthea, and how his apparently hopeless situation is at last happily resolved by the discovery that Panthea is, after all, *not* his sister. Prior to this fifth-act clarification, Arbaces delivers a number of violent speeches expressing thwarted lust, and one of these Yeats has quoted. Speaking of the words " brother " and " sister," which are the obstacles to his seemingly guilty passion, Arbaces cries, " Let 'em be anything but merely voice "—meaning that if only they were not bodiless words, but concrete things like soldiers or cities, he could turn his cannon on them and destroy them.

Yeats is comparing King Arbaces' frustrated desires to his own, and he is also comparing the words " brother " and " sister," which so vex Arbaces, to some unshakeable pledge or vow made by the lady who is the addressee of his poem. If we look into Richard Ellmann's biography of Yeats, we find that Maud Gonne, in 1909, had informed Yeats " that their relations could be those of a spiritual marriage only," and that she had assured him, "You will not suffer because I will pray." Once we have this information, Yeats' poem becomes perfectly clear: it is a plea for physical as well as spiritual love, and in re-reading it we must put a strong emphasis on the word "body" in the last line.

When one has managed to figure out some puzzling poem, it is natural to be a little foolishly proud; one feels like an insider, an initiate, and one is not inclined to be very critical of a work which has certified one's cleverness and industry. For a few heady weeks in 1954, I thought of myself as the only living understander of Yeats' "King and No King." Since then, however, the number of insiders has grown considerably, and I now feel less proprietary toward the poem, and more objective. There is much to admire in "King and No King": the rhythmic movement is splendidly dramatic; the language slides deftly in and out of the common idiom; in respect of pacing and diction, the poem is a good specimen of that artful recklessness, that *sprezzatura*, which Yeats was aiming at in the first decade of this century. Yet what an inconsistency there is between the blurting, spontaneous manner of the opening lines, and the poet's stubborn withholding of the theme! A good poet knows how, in referring to some little-known thing, to convey without loss of concision some sense of what the reference *must* mean; but Yeats, though he devotes almost seven lines to the Beaumont and Fletcher play, chooses to suppress any suggestion whatever that the play, and his poem, are concerned with frustrated sexual appetite. The consequence is that the reader stumbles badly on the sill of the poem, and never stops staggering until he is out the back door.

There are reasons, I suspect, for Yeats' having used a remote literary reference not only as a source of analogies to his personal predicament, but also as a means of enshrouding his subject matter. The subject is, after all, inherently delicate, and there is also some danger of the ridiculous in an argumentative plea for physical favors, especially if one has known the woman since the late 1880's. But whatever Yeats' reasons for writing as he did—and I have no real business guessing at them—one must wonder about the public value of a poem which mutes its theme by a thoroughly reticent allusion to a little-known text. One must also question the integrity, the artistic self-sufficiency, of any short poem which requires to be grasped through the reading of a bad five-act play and the consultation of a biography.

As the English critic John Press recently said, "There is a popular belief that what conservatives like to call real poetry was perfectly straightforward until some unspecified date, when poets suddenly changed into reckless bunglers or deliberately set out to bamboozle plain, honest readers with mumbo-jumbo." I hope that I don't seem to be offering aid and comfort to the holders of that unhistorical belief. What I do mean to say, in concession to Mr. Shapiro's view of things, is that the art of reference in poetry has become a very difficult art, owing to the incoherence of our culture, and that some poems refer more successfully than others. It is generally agreed, I hope, that one cannot sensibly describe a poem as a direct message from poet to public; but one can say that a poem addresses itself, in I. A. Richards' phrase, to some "condition of the language," and presupposes some condition of the culture. Every poem is based on an unformulated impression of what words and things are known and valued in the literate community; every poem is written, as it were, in some intellectual and cultural key. It is therefore possible to say of a poem that, in relation to its appropriate audience, it is tactful or not.

Housman's poem is a model of tact, both in its references and in its manner of referring. Yeats' poem is less tactful, because it cites an ancient play which the most eligible and cultured reader might not know, and which must be known if the poem is to be breached at all. As for the *Cantos* of Ezra Pound, they contain some of the finest passages in modern poetry, but they are supremely tactless. That is, they seem to arise from a despair of any community, and they do not imply a possible audience as Housman's poem does. It is all very well for Pound to claim that his *Cantos* deal " with the usual subjects of conversation between intelligent men "; but intelligent men, though they do talk of history and economics and the arts, do not converse in broken fragments of mythology, unattributed quotations, snatches of Renaissance correspondence, cryptic reminiscences, and bursts of unorthodox Chinese. Pound's presentational manner of writing, which developed out of Imagism, is the method least capable of turning his eccentric erudition into a consistently usable poetry. The advantage of the method is immediacy, and the investment of the idea in the thing, but the method does not work unless the reader knows what it is that is being so immediate. Because the *Cantos* lack any discursive tissue, because they refuse the reader any sort of intercession, even those whose learning exceeds Ezra Pound's cannot be said to be ready for them.

There are three things a reader might do about the *Cantos*. First, he might decide not to read them. Second, he might read them as Dr. Williams recommends, putting up with much bafflement for the sake of the occasional perfect lyric, the consistently clean and musical language, and the masterly achievement of quantitative effects through the strophic balancing of rhythmic masses. Or, thirdly, the reader might decide to understand the

Cantos by consulting, over a period of years, the many books from which Pound drew his material. At almost every university, nowadays, there is someone who has undertaken that task: he may be identified by the misshapenness of his learning and by his air of lost identity.

None of the three courses I have mentioned is a thoroughly happy one, and the *Cantos* are one proof of Mr. Shapiro's contention that poetry's relations with the past, on the one hand, and with its public on the other, have become problematical. I will grant Mr. Shapiro that there are misuses of the past which can be hurtful to poetry. Antiquarianism is one: the rapt pedantry of Ezra Pound, and the bland, donnish pedantry of certain other poets, alike distract us from the uninterpreted fields and streets and rooms of the present, in which the real battles of imagination must be fought. I will grant, too, that the sense of history can be crippling to poetry if history is so interpreted as to impose some narrow limitation or imperative on the poet. The poet must not feel dwarfed by the literary past, nor should he listen too trustingly to those who say that poetry's role in society is inevitably diminishing. Nor should he adjust his concerns to what others consider the great thought-currents of the times: the *Zeitgeist*, after all, is only a spook invented by the critics. Nor, finally, does poetry prosper when it puts itself wholly at the service of some movement, some institution. I think of Mayakovsky, who wrote "I have subdued myself, setting my heel on the throat of my own song," and who said that he had "cancelled out his soul" the better to serve the socialist age. It may be true, as some say, that Mayakovsky was made by the Revolution; but surely the service of history broke him as well. In all these ways, historical consciousness can paralyze, trivialize or enslave the poet's art; but I am not on that account moved to accept Mr. Shapiro's imperative, which is that poets must now secede from history and dwell in "biological time."

The past which most properly concerns the poet is, as T. S. Eliot has said, both temporal and timeless. It is, above all, a great index of human possibilities. It is a dimension in which we behold, and are beheld by, all those forms of excellence and depravity which men have assumed and may assume again. The poet needs this lively past as a means of viewing the present without provinciality, and of saying much in little; he must hope for the tact and the talent to make that past usable for the audience which his poems imply. My friend John Ciardi once said, "Pompeii is everybody's home town, sooner or later." I should add that for every poet, whatever he may say as critic or polemicist, Pompeii is still a busy quarter of the city of imagination.

Randall Jarrell

Robert Frost's
"Home Burial"

"HOME BURIAL" AND "THE Witch of Coös" seem to me the best of all Frost's dramatic poems—though "A Servant to Servants" is nearly as good. All three are poems about women in extreme situations: neurotic or (in "A Servant to Servants") psychotic women. The circumstances of the first half of his life made Frost feel for such women a sympathy or empathy that amounted almost to identification. He said that, "creature of literature that I am," he had learned to "make a virtue of my suffering / From nearly everything that goes on round me," and that "Kit Marlowe taught me how to say my prayers: / 'Why, this is Hell, nor am I out of it.'" It is with such women that he says this—this and more than this: the Pauper Witch of Grafton's

> Up where the trees grow short, the mosses tall,
> I made him gather me wet snow berries
> On slippery rocks beside a waterfall.
> I made him do it for me in the dark.
> And he liked everything I made him do . . .

shows us, as few passages can, that for a while the world was heaven too.

99

"Home Burial" is a fairly long but extraordinarily concentrated poem; after you have known it long enough you feel almost as the Evangelist did, that if all the things that could be said about it were written down, "I suppose that even the world itself could not contain the books that should be written." I have written down a few of these things; but, first of all, here is "Home Burial" itself:

> He saw her from the bottom of the stairs
> Before she saw him. She was starting down,
> Looking back over her shoulder at some fear.
> She took a doubtful step and then undid it
> To raise herself and look again. He spoke
> Advancing toward her: "What is it you see
> From up there always—for I want to know."
> She turned and sank upon her skirts at that,
> And her face changed from terrified to dull.
> He said to gain time: "What is it you see,"
> Mounting until she cowered under him.
> "I will find out now—you must tell me, dear."
> She, in her place, refused him any help
> With the least stiffening of her neck and silence.
> She let him look, sure that he wouldn't see,
> Blind creature; and awhile he didn't see.
> But at last he murmured, "Oh," and again, "Oh."
>
> "What is it—what?" she said.
>   "Just that I see."
>
> "You don't," she challenged. "Tell me what it is."
>
> "The wonder is I didn't see at once.
> I never noticed it from here before.
> I must be wonted to it—that's the reason.
> The little graveyard where my people are!
> So small the window frames the whole of it.
> Not so much larger than a bedroom, is it?

There are three stones of slate and one of marble,
Broad-shouldered little slabs there in the sunlight
On the sidehill. We haven't to mind *those*.
But I understand: it is not the stones,
But the child's mound—"

                      "Don't, don't, don't, don't," she cried.

She withdrew shrinking from beneath his arm
That rested on the banister, and slid downstairs;
And turned on him with such a daunting look,
He said twice over before he knew himself:
"Can't a man speak of his own child he's lost?"

"Not you! Oh, where's my hat? Oh, I don't need it!
I must get out of here. I must get air.
I don't know rightly whether any man can."

"Amy! Don't go to someone else this time.
Listen to me. I won't come down the stairs."
He sat and fixed his chin between his fists.
"There's something I should like to ask you, dear."

"You don't know how to ask it."

                         "Help me, then."

Her fingers moved the latch for all reply.

"My words are nearly always an offence.
I don't know how to speak of anything
So as to please you. But I might be taught,
I should suppose. I can't say I see how.
A man must partly give up being a man
With women-folk. We could have some arrangement
By which I'd bind myself to keep hands off
Anything special you're a-mind to name.
Though I don't like such things 'twixt those that love.
Two that don't love can't live together without them.
But two that do can't live together with them."
She moved the latch a little. "Don't—don't go.
Don't carry it to someone else this time.

Tell me about it if it's something human.
Let me into your grief. I'm not so much
Unlike other folks as your standing there
Apart would make me out. Give me my chance.
I do think, though, you overdo it a little.
What was it brought you up to think it the thing
To take your mother-loss of a first child
So inconsolably—in the face of love.
You'd think his memory might be satisfied—"

"There you go sneering now!"

                              "I'm not, I'm not!
You make me angry. I'll come down to you.
God, what a woman! And it's come to this,
A man can't speak of his own child that's dead."

"You can't because you don't know how to speak.
If you had any feelings, you that dug
With your own hand—how could you?—his little grave;
I saw you from that very window there
Making the gravel leap and leap in air,
Leap up, like that, like that, and land so lightly
And roll back down the mound beside the hole.
I thought, Who is that man? I didn't know you.
And I crept down the stairs and up the stairs
To look again, and still your spade kept lifting.
Then you came in. I heard your rumbling voice
Out in the kitchen, and I don't know why,
But I went near to see with my own eyes.
You could sit there with the stains on your shoes
Of the fresh earth from your own baby's grave
And talk about your everyday concerns.
You had stood the spade up against the wall
Outside there in the entry, for I saw it."

"I shall laugh the worst laugh I ever laughed.
I'm cursed. God, if I don't believe I'm cursed."

"I can repeat the very words you were saying.
'Three foggy mornings and one rainy day
Will rot the best birch fence a man can build.'
Think of it, talk like that at such a time!
What had how long it takes a birch to rot
To do with what was in the darkened parlor.
You *couldn't* care! The nearest friends can go
With anyone to death, comes so far short
They might as well not try to go at all.
No, from the time when one is sick to death,
One is alone, and he dies more alone.
Friends make pretense of following to the grave,
But before one is in it, their minds are turned
And making the best of their way back to life
And living people, and things they understand.
But the world's evil. I won't have grief so
If I can change it. Oh, I won't, I won't!"

"There, you have said it all and you feel better.
You won't go now. You're crying. Close the door.
The heart's gone out of it: why keep it up.
Amy! There's someone coming down the road!"

"*You*—oh, you think the talk is all. I must go—
Somewhere out of this house. How can I make you—"

"If—you—do!" She was opening the door wider.
"Where do you mean to go? First tell me that.
I'll follow and bring you back by force. I *will!*—"

The poem's first sentence, "He saw her from the bottom of the stairs / Before she saw him," implies what the poem very soon states: that, knowing herself seen, she would have acted differently—she has two sorts of behavior, behavior for him to observe and spontaneous immediate behavior. "She was starting down, / Looking back over her shoulder at some fear" says that it is *some fear*, and not a specific feared object, that she is looking back at; and, normally, we do not look back over our shoulder at what we leave, unless we feel for it something more than fear. "She took a doubtful step" emphasizes the queer attraction or fascination that the fear has for her; her departing step is not sure it should depart. "She took a doubtful step and then *undid* it": the surprising use of *undid* gives her withdrawal of the tentative step a surprising reality. The poem goes on: 'To raise herself and look again." It is a little vertical ballet of indecision toward and away from a fearful but mesmerically attractive object, something hard to decide to leave and easy to decide to return to. "He spoke / Advancing toward her": having the old line end with "spoke," the new line begin with "advancing," makes the very structure of the lines express the way in which he looms up, gets bigger. (Five lines later Frost repeats the effect even more forcibly with: "He said to gain time, 'What is it you see,' / Mounting until she cowered under him.") Now when the man asks: "What is it you see / From up there always—for I want to know," the word "always" tells us that all this has gone on many times before, and that he has seen it—without speaking of it—a number of times before. The phrase "for I want to know" is a characteristic example of the heavy, willed demands that the man makes, and an even more characteristic example of the tautological, rhetorical announcements of his actions that he so often makes, as if he felt that the announcement somehow justified or excused the action.

The poem goes on: "She turned and sank upon her skirts at that . . ." The stairs permit her to subside into a modest, compact, feminine bundle; there is a kind of smooth deftness about the phrase, as if it were some feminine saying: "When in straits, sink upon your skirts." The next line, "And her face changed from terrified to dull," is an economically elegant way of showing how the terror of surprise (perhaps with another fear underneath it) changes into the dull lack of response that is her regular mask for him. The poem continues: "He said to gain time"—to gain time in which to think of the next thing to say, to gain time in which to get close to her and gain the advantage of his physical nearness, his physical bulk. His next "What is it you see" is the first of his many repetitions; if one knew only this man one would say, "Man is the animal that repeats." In the poem's next phrase, "mounting until she cowered under him," the identity of the vowels in "mounting" and "cowered" physically connects the two, makes his mounting the plain immediate cause of her cowering. "I will find out now" is another of his rhetorical announcements of what he is going to do: "this time you're going to tell me, I'm going to make you." But this heavy willed compulsion changes into sheer appeal, into reasonable beseeching, in his next phrase: "You must tell me, dear." The "dear" is affectionate intimacy, the "must" is the "must" of rational necessity; yet the underlying form of the sentence is that of compulsion. The poem goes on: "She, in her place, refused him any help . . ." The separated phrase "in her place" describes and embodies, with economical brilliance, both her physical and spiritual lack of outgoingness, forthcomingness; she brims over none of her contours, remains sitting upon her skirts upon her stair-step, in feminine exclusion. "Refused him any help / With the least stiffening of her neck and silence": she doesn't say Yes, doesn't say No, doesn't say; her refusal of any answer is worse than almost any answer. "The least stiffening of her neck," in its concise reserve, its slight precision, is more nearly conclusive than any larger gesture of rejection. He, in extremities, usually repeats some proverbial or rhetorical generalization; at such moments she usually responds either with a particular, specific sentence, or else with something more particular than any sentence: with some motion or gesture.

The next line, " She let him look, sure that he wouldn't see,"
reminds one of some mother bird so certain that her nest is
hidden that she doesn't even flutter off, but sits there on it,
risking what is no risk, in complacent superiority. " Sure that
he wouldn't see, / Blind creature ": the last phrase is quoted
from her mind, is her contemptuous summing up. " And a while
he didn't see "; but at last when he sees, he doesn't tell her what
it is, doesn't silently understand, but with heavy slow comprehension murmurs, " Oh," and then repeats, " Oh." It is another
announcement of what he is doing, a kind of dramatic rendition
of his understanding. (Sometimes when we are waiting for
someone, and have made some sound or motion we are afraid
will seem ridiculous to the observer we didn't know was there,
we rather ostentatiously look at our watch, move our face and
lips into a " What on earth could have happened to make him
so late? " as a way of justifying our earlier action. The principle behind our action is the principle behind many of this
man's actions.) With the undignified alacrity of someone hurry-
ing to re-establish a superiority that has been questioned, the
woman cries out like a child: " What it is—what? " Her sentence
is, so to speak, a rhetorical question rather than a real one, since
it takes it for granted that a correct answer can't be made. His
reply, " Just that I see," shows that his unaccustomed insight
has given him an unaccustomed composure; she has had the
advantage, for so long, of being the only one who knows, that
he for a moment prolongs the advantage of being the only one
who knows that he knows. The immediately following " ' You
don't,' she challenged. ' Tell me what it is,' " is the instant,
childishly assertive exclamation of someone whose human position depends entirely upon her knowing what some inferior
being can never know; she cannot let another second go by

without hearing the incorrect answer that will confirm her in her rightness and superiority.

The man goes on explaining, to himself, and to mankind, and to her too, in slow rumination about it and about it. In his "The wonder is I didn't see at once. / I never noticed it from here before. / I must be wonted to it—that's the reason," one notices how "wonder" and "once" prepare for "wonted," that provincial-, archaic-sounding word that sums up—as "used" never could—his reliance on a habit or accustomedness which at last sees nothing but itself, and hardly sees that; and when it does see something through itself, beyond itself, slowly marvels. In the next line, "The little graveyard where my people are!" we feel not only the triumph of the slow person at last comprehending, but also the tender, easy accustomedness of habit, of long use, of a kind of cosy social continuance—for him the graves are not the healed scars of old agonies, but are something as comfortable and accustomed as the photographs in the family album. "So small the window frames the whole of it," like the later "Broad-shouldered little slabs there in the sunlight / On the sidehill," not only has this easy comfortable acceptance, but also has the regular feel of a certain sort of Frost nature-description: this is almost the only place in the poem where for a moment we feel that it is Frost talking first and the man talking second. But the man's "Not so much larger than a bedroom, is it?"—an observation that appeals to her for agreement—carries this comfortable acceptance to a point at which it becomes intolerable: the only link between the bedroom and the graveyard is the child conceived in their bedroom and buried in that graveyard. The sentence comfortably establishes a connection which she cannot bear to admit the existence of—she tries to keep the two things permanently separated in her mind. (What he says amounts to his saying about their bedroom:

"Not so much smaller than the graveyard, is it?") "There are three stones of slate and one of marble, / Broad-shouldered little slabs there in the sunlight / On the sidehill," has a heavy tenderness and accustomedness about it, almost as if he were running his hand over the grain of the stone. The "little" graveyard and "little" slabs are examples of our regular way of making something acceptable or dear by means of a diminutive.

Next, to show her how well he understands, the man shows her how ill he understands. He says about his family's graves: "We haven't to mind *those*"; that is, we don't have to worry about, grieve over, my people: it is not your obligation to grieve for them at all, nor mine to give them more than their proper share of grief, the amount I long ago measured out and used up. But with the feeling, akin to a sad, modest, relieved, surprised pride, with which he regularly responds to his own understanding, he tells her that he does understand: what matters is not the old stones but the new mound, the displaced earth piled up above the grave which he had dug and in which their child is buried.

When he says this it is as if he had touched, with a crude desecrating hand, the sacred, forbidden secret upon which her existence depends. With shuddering hysterical revulsion she cries: "Don't, don't, don't, don't." (If the reader will compare the effect of Frost's four "don'ts" with the effect of three or five, he will see once more how exactly accurate, perfectly effective, almost everything in the poem is.) The poem continues: "She withdrew shrinking from beneath his arm / That rested on the banister, and slid downstairs"; the word "slid" says, with vivid indecorousness, that anything goes in extremities, that you can't be bothered, then, by mere appearance or propriety; "slid" has the ludicrous force of actual fact, is the way things are instead of the way we agree they are. In the line "And turned on him with such a daunting look," the phrase "turned on him" makes her resemble a cornered animal turning on its pursuer; and "with such a daunting look" is the way he phrases it to himself, is quoted from his mind as "blind creature" was quoted from hers. The beautifully provincial, old-fashioned, folk-sounding "daunting" reminds one of the similar, slightly earlier "wonted," and seems to make immediate, as no other word could, the look that cows him. The next line, "He said twice over before he knew himself," tells us that repetition, saying something twice over, is something he regresses to under stress; unless he can consciously prevent himself from repeating, he repeats. What he says twice over (this is the third time already that he has repeated something) is a rhetorical question, a querulous, plaintive appeal to public opinion: "Can't a man speak of his own child he's lost?" He does not say specifically, particularly, with confidence in himself: "I've the right to speak of our dead child"; instead he cites the acknowledged fact that any member of the class *man* has the acknowledged right to mention, just to mention, that member of the class of his belongings, *his own child*—and he has been unjustly deprived of this right. "His own child he's lost" is a way of saying: "You act as if he were just yours, but he's just as much just mine; that's an established fact." "Can't a man speak of his own child he's lost" has a magnificently dissonant, abject, aggrieved querulousness about it, in all its sounds and all its rhythms; "Can't a man" prepares us for the even more triumphantly ugly dissonance (or should I say consonance?) of the last two words in her "I don't know rightly whether any man can."

Any rhetorical question demands, expects, the hearer's automatic agreement; there is nothing it expects less than a particular, specific denial. The man's "Can't a man speak . . ." means "Isn't any man allowed to speak . . . ," but her fatally specific answer, " Not you! " makes it mean, " A man cannot—is not able to—speak, if the man is you." Her " Oh, where's my hat? " is a speech accompanied by action, means: " I'm leaving. Where's the hat which social convention demands that a respectable woman put on, to go out into the world? " The immediately following " Oh, I don't need it! " means: in extremities, in cases when we come down to what really matters, what does social convention or respectability really matter? Her " I must get out of here. I must get air," says that you breathe understanding and suffocate without it, and that in this house, for her, there is none. Then, most extraordinarily, she gives a second specific answer to his rhetorical question, that had expected none: " I don't know rightly whether any man can." The line says: " Perhaps it is not the individual *you* that's to blame, but man in general; perhaps a woman is wrong to expect that any man can speak—really *speak*—of his dead child."

His " Amy! Don't go to someone else this time " of course tells us that another time she *has* gone to someone else; and it tells us the particular name of this most particular woman, something that she and the poem never tell us about the man. The man's " Listen to me. I won't come down the stairs " tells us that earlier he *has* come down the stairs, hasn't kept his distance. It (along with " shrinking," " cowered," and many later things in the poem) tells us that he has given her reason to be physically afraid of him; his " I won't come down the stairs " is a kind of euphemism for " I won't hurt you, won't even get near you."

The poem's next sentence, " He sat and fixed his chin between his fists "—period, end of line—with its four short *i*'s, its " fixed " and " fists," fixes him in baffled separateness; the sentence fits into the line as he fits into the isolated perplexity of his existence. Once more he makes a rhetorical announcement of what he is about to do, before he does it: " There's something I should

like to ask you, dear." The sentence tiptoes in, gentle, almost
abjectly mollifying, and ends with a reminding " dear"; it is
an indirect rhetorical appeal that expects for an answer at least
a grudging: "Well, go ahead and ask it, then." His sentence
presupposes the hearer's agreement with what it implies: "Anyone is at least allowed to *ask*, even if afterward you refuse him
what he asks." The woman once more gives a direct, crushing,
particular answer: "You don't know how to ask it." "Anyone
may be allowed to ask, but *you* are not because you are not able
to ask"; we don't even need to refuse an animal the right to
ask and be refused, since if we gave him the right he couldn't
exercise it. The man's "Help me, then," has an absolute,
almost abject helplessness, a controlled childlike simplicity,
that we pity and sympathize with; yet we can't help remem-
bering the other side of the coin, the heavy, brutal, equally
simple and helpless anger of his later *I'll come down to you.*

The next line, "Her fingers moved the latch for all reply"
(like the earlier "She refused him any help / With the least
stiffening of her neck and silence"; like "She turned on him
with such a daunting look"; like the later "She moved the latch
a little"; like the last "She was opening the door wider"),
reminds us that the woman has a motion-language more immediate, direct, and particular than words—a language she resorts
to in extremities, just as he, in extremities, resorts to a language
of repeated proverbial generalizations. "Home Burial" starts
on the stairs but continues in the doorway, on the threshold
between the old life inside and the new life outside.

The man now begins his long appeal with the slow, heavy,
hopeless admission that "My words are nearly always an offence."
This can mean, "Something is nearly always wrong with me
and my words," but it also can mean—does mean, underneath—
that she is to be blamed for nearly always finding offensive

things that certainly are not meant to offend. "I don't know how to speak of anything / So as to please you" admits, sadly blames himself for, his baffled ignorance, but it also suggests that she is unreasonably, fantastically hard to please—if the phrase came a little later in his long speech he might pronounce it "so as to please *you*." (Whatever the speaker intends, there are no long peacemaking speeches in a quarrel; after a few sentences the speaker always has begun to blame the other again.) The man's aggrieved, blaming "But I might be taught, I should suppose" is followed by the helpless, very endearing admission: "I can't say I see how"; for the moment this removes the blame from her, and his honesty of concession makes us unwilling to blame him. He tries to summarize his dearly-bought understanding in a generalization, almost a proverb: "A man must partly give up being a man / With women-folk." The sentence begins in the dignified regretful sunlight of the main floor, in "A man must partly give up being a man," and ends huddled in the basement below, in "With women-folk." He doesn't use the parallel, co-ordinate "with a woman," but the entirely different "with women-folk"; the sentence tries to be fair and objective, but it is as completely weighted a sentence as "A man must partly give up being a man / With the kiddies," or "A man must partly give up being a man / With Bandar-log." The sentence presupposes that the real right norm is a man being a man with men, and that some of this rightness and normality always must be sacrificed with that special case, that inferior anomalous category, "women-folk."

He goes on: "We could have some arrangement [it has a hopeful, indefinite, slightly helter-skelter sound] / By which I'd bind myself to keep hands off"—the phrases "bind myself" and "keep hands off" have the primitive, awkward materiality of someone taking an oath in a bad saga; we expect the sentence to end in some awkwardly impressive climax, but get the almost ludicrous anticlimax of "Anything special you're a-mind to name." And, too, the phrase makes whatever she names quite willful on her part, quite unpredictable by reasonable man. His sensitivity usually shows itself to be a willing, hopeful form of insensitivity, and he himself realizes this here, saying: "Though I don't like such things 'twixt those that love." Frost then makes him express his own feeling in a partially truthful but elephantine aphorism that lumbers, through a queerly stressed line a foot too long ("Two that don't love can't live together without them") into a conclusion ("But two that do can't live together with them") that has some of the slow, heavy relish just in being proverbial that the man so often shows. (How hard it is to get through the monosyllables of the two lines!) His words don't convince her, and she replies to them without words: "She moved the latch a little." He repeats in grieved appeal: "Don't—don't go. / Don't carry it to someone else this time." (He is repeating an earlier sentence, with "don't go" changed to "don't carry it.") The next line, "Tell me about it if it's something human," is particularly interesting when it comes from him. When is something inside a human being not human, so that it can't be told? Isn't it when it is outside man's understanding, outside all man's categories and pigeonholes—when there is no proverb to say for it? It is, then, a waste or abyss impossible to understand or manage or share with another. His next appeal to her, "Let me into your grief," combines an underlying sexual metaphor with a child's "Let me in! let me in!" This man who is so much a member of the human community feels a helpless bewilderment at being shut out of the little group of two of which he was once an anomalous half; the woman has put in the place of this group, a group of herself-and-the-dead-child, and he begs or threatens—reasons with her as best he can—in his attempt to get her to restore the first group, so that there will be a man-and-wife grieving over their dead child.

He goes on: "I'm not so much / Unlike other folks as your standing there / Apart would make me out." The "standing there / Apart" is an imitative, expressive form that makes her apart, shows her apart. Really her apartness makes him out *like* other folks, all those others who make pretense of following to the grave, but who before one's back is turned have made their way back to life; but he necessarily misunderstands her, since for him being like others is necessarily good, being unlike them necessarily bad. His "Give me my chance"—he doesn't say *a* chance—reminds one of those masculine things fairness and sportsmanship, and makes one think of the child's demand for justice, equal shares, which follows his original demand for exclusive possession, the lion's share. "Give me my chance" means: "You, like everybody else, must admit that anybody deserves a chance—so give me mine"; he deserves his chance not by any particular qualities, personal merit, but just by virtue of being a human being. His "I do think, though, you overdo it a little" says that he is forced against his will to criticize her for so much exceeding (the phrase "a little" is understatement, politeness, and caution) the norm of grief, for mourning more than is usual or reasonable; the phrase "overdo it a little" manages to reduce her grief to the level of a petty social blunder. His next words, "What was it brought you up to think it the thing / To take your mother-loss of a first child / So inconsolably—in the face of love," manage to crowd four or five kinds of condemnation into a single sentence. "What was it brought you up" says that it is not your essential being but your accidental upbringing that has made you do this—it reduces the woman to a helpless social effect. "To think it the thing" is particularly insulting because it makes her grief a mere matter of fashion; it is as though he were saying, "What was it brought you up to think it the thing / To wear your skirt that far above your knees?" The phrase "to take your mother-loss of a first child" pigeonholes her loss, makes it a regular, predictable category that demands a regular, predictable amount of grief, and no more. The phrase "so inconsolably—in the face of love" condemns her for being so unreasonable as not to be consoled by, for paying no attention to, that unarguably good, absolutely general thing, love; the generalized *love* makes demands upon her that are inescapable, compared to those which would be made by a more specific phrase like "in the face of my love for you." The man's "You'd think his memory might be satisfied" again condemns her for exceeding the reasonable social norm of grief; condemns her, jealously, for mourning as if the dead child's demands for grief were insatiable.

Her interruption, "There you go sneering now!" implies that he has often before done what she calls "sneering" at her and her excessive sensitivity; and, conscious of how hard he has been trying to make peace, and unconscious of how much his words have gone over into attack, he contradicts her like a child, in righteous anger: "I'm not, I'm not!" His "You make me angry" is another of his rhetorical, tautological announcements about himself, one that is intended somehow to justify the breaking of his promise not to come down to her; he immediately makes the simple childish threat, "I'll come down to you"— he is repeating his promise, "I won't come down to you," with the "not" removed. "God, what a woman!" righteously and despairingly calls on God and public opinion (that voice of the people which is the voice of God) to witness and marvel at what he is being forced to put up with: the fantastic, the almost unbelievable wrongness and unreasonableness of this woman.

" And it's come to this," that regular piece of rhetorical recrimina-
tion in quarrels, introduces his *third* use of the sentence " Can't
a man speak of his own child he's lost"; but this time the
rhetorical question is changed into the factual condemnation
of "A man can't speak of his own child that's dead." This
time he doesn't end the sentence with the more sentimental,
decorous, sympathy-demanding " that's lost," but ends with the
categorical " that's dead."

Earlier the woman has given two entirely different, entirely
specific and unexpected answers to this rhetorical question of
his; this time she has a third specific answer, which she makes
with monosyllabic precision and finality: " You can't because
you don't know how to speak." He has said that it is an awful
thing not to be permitted to speak of his own dead child; she
replies that it is not a question of permission but of ability, that
he is too ignorant and insensitive to be *able* to speak of his
child. Her sentence is one line long, and it is only the second
sentence of hers that has been that long. He has talked at
length during the first two-thirds of the poem, she in three-
or four-word phrases or in motions without words; for the rest
of the poem she talks at length, as everything that has been
shut up inside her begins to pour out. She opens herself up,
now—is far closer to him, striking at him with her words, than
she has been sitting apart, in her place. His open attack has
finally elicited from her, by contagion, her open anger, so that
now he is something real and unbearable to attack, instead of
being something less-than-human to be disregarded.

This first sentence has indicted him; now she brings in the
specific evidence for the indictment. She says: " If you had any
feelings, you that dug / With your own hand "—but after the
three stabbing, indicting stresses of

/ / /
your own hand

she breaks off the sentence, as if she found the end unbearable to go on to; interjects, her throat tightening, the incredulous rhetorical question, "how could you?"—and finishes with the fact that she tries to make more nearly endurable, more euphemistic, with the tender word "little": "his little grave." The syntax of the sentence doesn't continue, but the fact of things continues; she says, "I saw you from that very window there."

That very window there

has the same stabbing stresses, the same emphasis on a specific, damning actuality, that

your own hand

had—and that, soon,

my own eyes

and

your own baby's grave

and other such phrases will have. She goes on: "Making the gravel leap and leap in air, / Leap up, like that, like that, and land so lightly / And roll back down the mound beside the hole." As the sentence imitates with such terrible life and accuracy the motion of the gravel, her throat tightens and aches in her hysterical repetition of "like that, like that": the sounds of "leap and leap in air, / Leap up like that, like that, and land so lightly" are "le! le! le! li! li! la! li!" and re-create the sustained hysteria she felt as she first watched; inanimate things, the very stones, leap and leap in air, or when their motion subsides land "so lightly," while the animate being, her dead child, does not move, will never move. (The foxes have holes, and the birds of the air have nests; but the Son of man hath not where to lay his head.) Her words "leap and leap in air, leap up, like that, like that" keep the stones alive! alive! alive!—in the words "and land" they start to die away, but the following words "so lightly" make them alive again, for a last moment of unbearable contradiction, before they "*roll* back *down* the *mound* beside the *hole.*" The repeated *o*'s (the line says "oh! ow! ow! oh!") make almost crudely actual the abyss of death into which the pieces of gravel and her child fall, not to rise again. The word "hole" (insisted on even more by the rhyme with "roll") gives to the grave the obscene actuality that watching the digging forced it to have for her.

She says: "I thought, Who is that man? I didn't know you." She sees the strange new meaning in his face (what, underneath, the face has meant all along) so powerfully that the face itself seems a stranger's. If her own husband can do something so impossibly alien to all her expectations, he has never really been anything but alien; all her repressed antagonistic knowledge about his insensitivity comes to the surface and masks what before had masked it. In the next sentence, "And I crept down the stairs and up the stairs / To look again," the word "crept" makes her a little mouselike thing crushed under the weight of her new knowledge. But the truly extraordinary word is the "and" that joins "down the stairs" to "up the stairs." What is so extraordinary is that she sees nothing extraordinary about it: the "and" joining the two co-ordinates hides from her, shows that she has repressed, the thoroughly illogical, contradictory nature of her action; it is like saying: "And I ran out of the fire and back into the fire," and seeing nothing strange about the sentence.

Her next words, "And still your spade kept lifting," give the man's tool a dead, mechanical life of its own; it keeps on and on, crudely, remorselessly, neither guided nor halted by spirit. She continues: "Then you came in. I heard your rumbling voice /

Out in the kitchen"; the word "rumbling" gives this great blind creature an insensate weight and strength that are, somehow, hollow. Then she says that she did something as extraordinary as going back up the stairs, but she masks it, this time, with the phrase "and I don't know why." She doesn't know why, it's unaccountable, "But I went near to see with my own eyes." Her "I don't know why" shows her regular refusal to admit things like these; she manages by a confession of ignorance not to have to make the connections, consciously, that she has already made unconsciously.

She now says a sentence that is an extraordinarily conclusive condemnation of him: "You could sit there with the stains on your shoes / Of the fresh earth from your own baby's grave / And talk about your everyday concerns." The five hissing or spitting s's in the strongly accented "sit," "stains," "shoes"; the whole turning upsidedown of the first line, with four trochaic feet followed by one poor iamb; the concentration of intense, damning stresses in

$$\acute{\text{fresh}} \; \acute{\text{earth}} \; \text{of} \; \acute{\text{your}} \; \acute{\text{own}} \; \acute{\text{baby's}} \; \acute{\text{grave}}$$

—all these things give an awful finality to the judge's summing-up, so that in the last line, "and talk about your everyday concerns," the criminal's matter-of-fact obliviousness has the perversity of absolute insensitivity: Judas sits under the cross matching pennies with the soldiers. The poem has brought to life an unthought-of literal meaning of its title: this is home burial with a vengeance, burial *in* the home; the fresh dirt of the grave stains her husband's shoes and her kitchen floor, and the dirty spade with which he dug the grave stands there in the entry. As a final unnecessary piece of evidence, a last straw that comes long after the camel's back is broken, she states: "You had stood the spade up against the wall / Outside there in the entry, for I saw it." All her pieces of evidence have written underneath them, like Goya's drawing, that triumphant, traumatic, unarguable I SAW IT.

The man's next sentence is a kind of summing-up-in-little of his regular behavior, the ways in which (we have come to see) he *has* to respond. He has begged her to let him into her grief, to tell him about it if it's something human; now she lets him into not her grief but her revolted, hating condemnation of him; she does tell him about it and it isn't human, but a nightmare into which he is about to fall. He says: " I shall laugh the worst laugh I ever laughed. / I'm cursed. God, if I don't believe I'm cursed." The sounds have the gasping hollowness of some-body hit in the stomach and trying over and over to get his breath—of someone nauseated and beginning to vomit: the first stressed vowel sounds are " agh! uh! agh! uh! agh! uh!" He doesn't reply to her, argue with her, address her at all, but makes a kind of dramatic speech that will exhibit him in a role public opinion will surely sympathize with, just as he sympathizes with himself. As always, he repeats: " laugh," " laugh," and " laugh," " I'm cursed" and " I'm cursed" (the rhyme with " worst" gives almost the effect of another repetition); as always, he announces beforehand what he is going to do, rhetorically appealing to mankind for justification and sympathy. His " I shall laugh the worst laugh I ever laughed" has the queer effect of seeming almost to be quoting some folk proverb. His " I'm cursed" manages to find a category of understanding in which to pigeonhole this nightmare, makes him a reasonable human being helpless against the inhuman powers of evil—the cursed one is not to blame. His " God, if I don't believe I'm cursed" is akin to his earlier " God, what a woman! "—both have some-thing of the male's outraged, incredulous, despairing response to the unreasonableness and immorality of the female. He responds hardly at all to the exact situation; instead he demands sympathy for, sympathizes with himself for, the impossibly unlucky pigeonhole into which Fate has dropped him.

His wife then repeats the sentence that, for her, sums up everything: "I can repeat the very words you were saying. / 'Three foggy mornings and one rainy day / Will rot the best birch fence a man can build.'" We feel with a rueful smile that he has lived by proverbs and—now, for her—dies by them. He has handled his fresh grief by making it a part of man's regular routine, man's regular work; and by quoting man's regular wisdom, that explains, explains away, pigeonholes, anything. Nature tramples down man's work, the new fence rots, but man still is victorious, in the secure summing-up of the proverb.

The bést bírch fénce

is, so far as its stresses are concerned, a firm, comfortable parody of all those stabbing stress-systems of hers. In his statement, as usual, it is not *I* but *a man*. There is a resigned but complacent, almost relishing wit about this summing-up of the transitoriness of human effort: to understand your defeat so firmly, so proverbially, is in a sense to triumph. He has seen his ordinary human ambition about that ordinary human thing, a child, frustrated by death; so there is a certain resignation and pathos about his saying what he says. The word "rot" makes the connection between the fence and the child, and it is the word "rot" that is unendurable to the woman, since it implies with obscene directness: how many foggy mornings and rainy days will it take to rot the best flesh-and-blood child a man can have? Just as, long ago at the beginning of the poem, the man brought the bedroom and the grave together, he brings the rotting child and the rotting fence together now. She says in incredulous, breathless outrage: "Think of it, talk like that at such a time!" (The repeated sounds, *th, t, t, th, t, t,* are thoroughly expressive.) But once more she has repressed the connection between the two things: she objects to the sentence not as what she knows it is, as rawly and tactlessly relevant, but as something absolutely irrelevant, saying: "What had how long it takes a birch to rot / To do with "—and then she puts in a euphemistic circumlocution, lowers her eyes and lowers the shades so as not to see—"what was in the darkened parlor."

But it is time to go back and think of just what it was the woman saw, just how she saw it, to make her keep on repeating that first occasion of its sight. She saw it on a holy and awful day. The child's death and burial were a great and almost unendurable occasion, something that needed to be accompanied with prayer and abstention, with real grief and the ritual expression of grief. It was a holy or holi-day that could only be desecrated by "everyday concerns"; the husband's digging seemed to the wife a kind of brutally unfeeling, secular profanation of that holy day, her holy grief. Her description makes it plain that her husband dug strongly and well. And why should he not do so? Grief and grave-digging, for him, are in separate compartments; the right amount of grief will never flow over into the next compartment. To him it is the workaday, matter-of-fact thing that necessarily comes first; grieving for the corpse is no excuse for not having plenty of food at the wake. If someone had said to him: "You dig mighty well for a man that's just lost his child," wouldn't he have replied: "Grief's no reason for doing a bad job"? (And yet, the muscles tell the truth; a sad enough man shovels badly.) When, the grave dug and the spade stood up in the entry, he went into the kitchen, he may very well have felt: "A good job," just as Yakov, in *Rothschild's Fiddle*, taps the coffin he has made for his wife and thinks: "A good job."

But unconsciously, his wife has far more compelling reasons to be appalled at this job her husband is doing. Let me make this plain. If we are told how a woman dreams of climbing the stairs, and of looking out through a window at a man digging a hole with a spade—digging powerfully, so that the gravel leaps and leaps into the air, only to roll back down into the hole; and still the man's spade keeps lifting and plunging down, lifting and plunging down, as she watches in fascinated horror, creeps down the stairs, creeps back up against her will, to keep on watching; and then, she doesn't know why, she has to go to see with her own eyes the fresh earth staining the man's shoes, has to see with her own eyes the man's tool stood up against the wall, in the entrance to the house—if we are told such a dream, is there any doubt what *sort* of dream it will seem to us? Such things have a sexual force, a sexual meaning, as much in our waking hours as in our dreams—as we know from how many turns of speech, religious rites, myths, tales, works of art. When the plowman digs his plow into the earth, Mother Earth, to make her bear, this does not have a sexual appropriateness only in the dreams of neurotic patients—it is something that we all understand, whether or not we admit that we understand. So the woman understood her husband's digging. If the spade, the tool that he stands up in the entry, stands for man's workaday world, his matter-of-fact objectivity and disregard of emotion, it also stands for his masculinity, his sexual power; on this holy day he brings back into the house of grief the soiling stains of fresh earth, of this digging that, to her, is more than digging.

That day of the funeral the grieving woman felt only misery and anguish, passive suffering; there was nobody to blame for it all except herself. And how often women do blame themselves for the abnormality or death of a baby! An old doctor says: they keep blaming themselves; they should have done this, that, something; they forget all about their husbands; often they blame some doctor who, by not coming immediately, by doing or not doing something, was responsible for it all: the woman's feeling of guilt about other things is displaced onto the child's death. Now when this woman sees her husband digging the grave (doing what seems to her, consciously, an intolerably insensitive thing; unconsciously, an indecent thing) she *does* have someone to blame, someone upon whom to shift her own guilt: she is able to substitute for passive suffering and guilt an active loathing and condemnation—as she blames the man's greater guilt and wrongness her own lesser guilt can seem in comparison innocence and rightness. (The whole matrix of attitudes available to her, about woman as Madonna-and-child and man as brute beast, about sexuality as a defiling thing forced upon woman, helps her to make this shift.) The poem has made it easy for us to suspect a partial antagonism or uncongeniality, sexually, between the weak oversensitive woman and the strong insensitive man, with his sexual force so easily transformed into menace. (The poem always treats it in that form.) The woman's negative attitudes have been overwhelmingly strengthened, now; it is plain that since the child's death there has been no sort of sexual or emotional union between them.

To her, underneath, the child's death must have seemed a punishment. Of whom for what? Of them for what they have done—sexual things are always tinged with guilt; but now her complete grief, her separateness and sexual and emotional abstention, help to cancel out her own guilt—the man's matter-of-fact physical obliviousness, his desire to have everything what it was before, reinforce his own guilt and help to make it seem absolute. Yet, underneath, the woman's emotional and physiological needs remain unchanged, and are satisfied by this compulsory symptomatic action of hers—this creeping up the stairs, looking, looking, creeping down and then back up again, looking, looking; she stares with repudiating horror, with accepting fascination, at this obscenely symbolic sight. It is not the child's mound she stares at, but the scene of the crime, the site of this terrible symbolic act that links sexuality and death, the marriage-bed and the grave. (Afterward she had gone down into the kitchen to see the man flushed and healthy, breathing a little harder after physical exertion; her words, "I heard your *rumbling* voice out in the kitchen," remind us of that first telling description of him on the stairs, "*mounting* until she *cowered* under him." Her first response to the sight, "I thought: Who *is* that man? I didn't know you," makes him not her husband but a stranger, a guilty one, whom she is right to remain estranged from, must remain estranged from.) Her repeated symptomatic act has the consciousness of obsessional-compulsive symptoms, not the un-consciousness of hysterical blindness or paralysis: she is conscious of what she is doing, knows how it all began; and yet she cannot keep from doing it, does not really know why she does it, and is conscious only of a part of the meaning it has for her. She has isolated it, and refuses to see its connections, consciously, because the connections are so powerful unconsciously: so that she says, "And I crept down the stairs *and* up the stairs"; says, "*And I don't know why,* / But I went near to see with my own eyes"; says, "What had how long it takes a birch to rot / To do with what was in the darkened parlor?"

This repeated symptomatic action of hers satisfies several needs. It keeps reassuring her that she is right to keep herself fixed in separation and rejection. By continually revisiting this scene, by looking again and again at—so to speak—this indecent photo-graph of her husband's crime, she is making certain that she will never come to terms with the criminal who, in the photo-

graph, is committing the crime. Yet, underneath, there is a part
of her that takes guilty pleasure in the crime, that is in identifying complicity with the criminal. A symptom or symptomatic
action is an expression not only of the defense against the forbidden wish, but also of the forbidden wish.

If the reader doubts that this symptomatic action of hers
has a sexual root, he can demonstrate it to himself by imagining
the situation different in one way. Suppose the wife had looked
out of the window and seen her husband animatedly and matter-
of-factly bargaining to buy a cemetery lot from one of the next
day's funeral guests. She would have been angered and revolted. But would she have crept back to look again? have gone
into the kitchen so as to see the bargainer with her own eyes?
have stared in fascination at the wallet from which he had taken
the money? Could she as easily have made a symptom of it?

After she has finished telling the story of what she had seen,
of what he had done, she cries: "You *couldn't* care!" The
words say: "If you could behave as you behaved it proves that
you didn't care and, therefore, that you couldn't care; if you,
my own husband, the child's own father, were unable to care,
it proves that it must be impossible for anyone to care." So she
goes on, not about him but about everyone: "The nearest
friends can go / With anyone to death, comes so far short /
They might as well not try to go at all." The sentence has some
of the rueful, excessive wit of Luther's "In every good act the
just man sins"; man can do so little he might as well do nothing.
Her next sentence, "No, from the time when one is sick to
death, / One is alone, and he dies more alone," tolls like a lonely
bell for the human being who grieves for death and, infected
by what she grieves for, dies alone in the pest house, deserted
by the humanity that takes good care not to be infected. When

you truly feel what death is, you must die: all her phrases about
the child's death and burial make them her own death and burial.

She goes on: "Friends make pretence of following to the
grave, / But before one is in it their minds are turned"—her
"make pretence" blames their, his, well-meant hypocrisy; her
"before one is in it" speaks of the indecent haste with which he
hurried to dig the grave into which the baby was put, depriving
her of it—of the indecent haste with which he forgot death and
wanted to resume life. The phrases "their minds are turned"
and "making the best of their way back" are (as so often with
Frost) queerly effective adaptations of ordinary idioms, of "their
backs are turned" and "making the best of things"; these are
the plain roots, in the woman's mind, of her less direct and more
elaborate phrases. But when we have heard her whole sentence:
"Friends make pretense of following to the grave / But before
one is in it their minds are turned / And making the best of
their way back to life / And living people, and things they understand," we reply: "As they must." She states as an evil what
we think at worst a necessary evil; she is condemning people for
not committing suicide, for not going down into the grave with
the corpse and dying there. She condemns the way of the world,
but it is the way of any world that continues to be a world: the
world that does otherwise perishes. Her "But the world's evil.
I won't have grief so / If I can change it. Oh, I won't, I won't!"
admits what grief is to everybody else; is generally; and says
that she will change the universal into her own contradictory
particular if she can: the sentence has its own defeat inside it.
What this grieving woman says about grief is analogous to a
dying woman's saying about death: "I won't have death so /
If I can change it. Oh, I won't, I won't!" Even the man responds to the despairing helplessness in her "Oh, I won't, I
won't!" She is still trying to be faithful and unchanging in her

grief, but already she has begun to be faithless, has begun to change. Saying, " I never have colds any more," an hour or two before one has a cold, is one's first unconscious recognition that one has caught cold; similarly, she says that other people forget and change but that she never will, just when she has begun to change—just when, by telling her husband the cause of her complete separation, she has begun to destroy the completeness of the separation. Her " Oh, I won't, I won't! " sounds helplessly dissolving, running-down; already contains within it the admission of what it denies. Her " I won't have grief so " reminds us that grief *is* so, is by its very nature a transition to something that isn't grief. She knows it too, so that she says that everybody else is that way, the world is that way, but they're wrong, they're evil; *someone* must be different; *someone* honorably and quixotically, at no matter what cost, must contradict the nature of grief, the nature of the world.

All this is inconceivable to the man: if everybody is that way, it must be right to be that way; it would be insanity to think of any other possibility. She has put grief, the dead child, apart on an altar, to be kept separate and essential as long as possible—forever, if possible. He has immediately filed away the child, grief, in the pigeonhole of man's wont, man's proverbial understanding: the weight is off his own separate shoulders, and the shoulders of all mankind bear the burden. In this disaster of her child's death, her husband's crime, her one consolation is that she is inconsolable, has (good sensitive woman) grieved for months as her husband (bad insensitive man) was not able to grieve even for hours. Ceasing to grieve would destroy this consolation, would destroy the only way of life she has managed to find.

And yet she has begun to destroy them. When she says at the end of the poem: " How can I make you—" understand, see, she shows in her baffled, longing despair that she *has* tried to make him understand; has tried to help him as he asked her to help him. Her "You *couldn't* care," all her lines about what friends and the world necessarily are, excuse him in a way, by making him a necessarily insensitive part of a necessarily insensitive world that she alone is sensitive in: she is the one person desperately and forlornly trying to be different from everyone else, as she tries to keep death and grief alive in the middle of a world intent on its own forgetful life. At these last moments she does not, as he thinks, "set him apart" as "so much unlike other folks"; if he could hear and respond to what she actually has said, there would be some hope for them. But he doesn't; instead of understanding her special situation, he dumps her into the pigeonhole of the crying woman—any crying woman—and then tries to *manage* her as one manages a child. She does try to let him into her grief, but he won't go; instead he tells her that now she's had her cry, that now she feels better, that the heart's gone out of it, that there's really no grief left for him to be let into.

The helpless tears into which her hard self-righteous separateness has dissolved show, underneath, a willingness to accept understanding; she has denounced him, made a clean breast of things, and now is accessible to the understanding or empathy that he is unable to give her. Women are oversensitive, exaggerate everything, tell all, weep, and then are all right: this is the pigeonhole into which he drops her. So rapid an understanding can almost be called a form of stupidity, of not even trying really to understand. The bewitched, uncanny, almost nauseated helplessness of what he has said a few lines before: "I shall laugh the worst laugh I ever laughed. / I'm cursed. God, if I don't believe I'm cursed," has already changed into a feeling of mastery, of the strong man understanding and managing the weak hysterical woman. He is the powerful one now. His "There, you have said it all and you feel better. You won't go now," has all the grownup's condescension toward the child, the grownup's ability to make the child do something simply by stating that the child is about to do it. The man's "You're crying. Close the door. / The heart's gone out of it: why keep it up," shows this quite as strikingly; he feels that he can manipulate her back into the house and into his life, back out of the grief that— he thinks or hopes—no longer has any heart in it, so that she must pettily and exhaustingly "keep it up."

But at this moment when the depths have been opened for him; at this moment when the proper management might get her back into the house, the proper understanding get her back into his life; at this moment that it is fair to call the most important moment of his life, someone happens to come down the road. Someone who will see her crying and hatless in the doorway; someone who will go back to the village and tell everything; someone who will shame them in the eyes of the world. Public opinion, what people will say, is more important to him than anything she will do; he forgets everything else, and expostulates: "Amy! There's someone coming down the road!" His exclamation is full of the tense, hurried fear of social impropriety, of public disgrace; nothing could show more forcibly what he *is* able to understand, what he *does* think of primary importance. Her earlier "Oh, where's my hat? Oh, I don't need it!" prepares for, is the exact opposite of, his "Amy! There's someone coming down the road!"

She says with incredulous, absolute intensity and particularity: "*You*—"

That italicized *you* is the worst, the most nearly final thing that she can say about him, since it merely points to what he is. She doesn't go on; goes back and replies to his earlier sentences: "oh, you think the talk is all." Her words have a despairing limpness and sadness: there is no possibility of his being made to think anything different, to see the truth under the talk. She says: "I must go—" and her words merely recognize a reality—"Somewhere out of this house." Her final words are full of a longing, despairing, regretful realization of a kind of final impossibility: "How can I make you—" The word that isn't said, that she stops short of saying, is as much there as anything in the poem. All her insistent anxious pride in her own separateness and sensitiveness and superiority is gone; she knows, now, that she is separate from him no matter what she wants. Her "How can I make you—" amounts almost to: "If only I could make you—if only there were some way to make you—but there is no way."

He responds not to what she says but to what she does, to "She was opening the door wider." He threatens, as a child would threaten: "If—you—do!" He sounds like a giant child, or a child being a giant or an ogre. The "If—you—do!" uses as its principle of being the exaggerated slowness and heaviness, the *willedness* of his nature. (Much about him reminds me of Yeats' famous definition: "Rhetoric is the will trying to do the work of the imagination"; "Home Burial" might be called the story of a marriage between the will and the imagination.) The dashes Frost inserts between the words slow down the words to the point where the slowedness or heaviness itself, as pure force and menace, is what is communicated. Then the man says, trying desperately—feebly—to keep her within reach of that force or menace: "Where do you mean to go? First tell me that. / I'll follow and bring you back by force. I *will!*" The last sentences of each of her previous speeches (her despairing emotional "Oh, I won't! I won't!" and her despairing spiritual "How can I make you—") are almost the exact opposite of the "I *will!*"

with which he ends the poem. It is appropriate that "force," "I," and "*will*" are his last three words: his proverbial, town-meeting understanding has failed, just as his blankly imploring humility has failed; so that he has to resort to the only thing he has left, the will or force that seems almost like the mass or inertia of a physical body. We say that someone "throws his weight around," and in the end there is nothing left for him to do but throw his weight around. Appropriately, his last line is one more rhetorical announcement of what he is going to do: he will follow and bring her back by force; and, appropriately, he ends the poem with one more repetition—he repeats: "I *will!*"

Author Index